Martin Van Buren

Ted Widmer

Martin
Van Buren

THE AMERICAN PRESIDENTS SERIES

ARTHUR M. SCHLESINGER, JR., GENERAL EDITOR

Times Books

HENRY HOLT AND COMPANY, NEW YORK

Times Books
Henry Holt and Company, LLC
Publishers since 1866
115 West 18th Street
New York, New York 10011

Henry Holt® is a registered trademark of Henry Holt and Company, LLC.

Library of Congress Cataloging-in-Publication Data
Widmer, Edward L.
    Martin Van Buren / Ted Widmer.—1st ed.
        p. cm.—(The American presidents)
    Includes bibliographical references and index.
    ISBN 0-8050-6922-4
    EAN 978-0-8050-6922-8
    1. Van Buren, Martin, 1782–1862. 2. Presidents—United States—Biography.
3. United States—Politics and government—1837–1841. I. Title. II. American
presidents series (Times Books (Firm))
    E397.W535 2005
    973.5'7'092—dc22   2004053652

Henry Holt books are available for special promotions and premiums.
For details contact: Director, Special Markets.

First Edition 2005

Printed in the United States of America
1 3 5 7 9 10 8 6 4 2

Contents

Editor's Note

THE AMERICAN PRESIDENCY

The president is the central player in the American political order. That would seem to contradict the intentions of the Founding Fathers. Remembering the horrid example of the British monarchy, they invented a separation of powers in order, as Justice Brandeis later put it, "to preclude the exercise of arbitrary power." Accordingly, they divided the government into three allegedly equal and coordinate branches—the executive, the legislative, and the judiciary.

But a system based on the tripartite separation of powers has an inherent tendency toward inertia and stalemate. One of the three branches must take the initiative if the system is to move. The executive branch alone is structurally capable of taking that initiative. The Founders must have sensed this when they accepted Alexander Hamilton's proposition in the Seventieth Federalist that "energy in the executive is a leading character in the definition of good government." They thus envisaged a strong president—but within an equally strong system of constitutional accountability. (The term *imperial presidency* arose in the 1970s to describe the situation when the balance between power and accountability is upset in favor of the executive.)

The American system of self-government thus comes to focus in the presidency—"the vital place of action in the system," as Woodrow Wilson put it. Henry Adams, himself the great-grandson and grandson of presidents as well as the most brilliant of American historians, said that the American president "resembles the commander of a ship at sea. He must have a helm to grasp, a course to steer, a port to seek." The men in the White House (thus far only men, alas) in steering their chosen courses have shaped our destiny as a nation.

Biography offers an easy education in American history, rendering the past more human, more vivid, more intimate, more accessible, more connected to ourselves. Biography reminds us that presidents are not supermen. They are human beings too, worrying about decisions, attending to wives and children, juggling balls in the air, and putting on their pants one leg at a time. Indeed, as Emerson contended, "There is properly no history; only biography."

Presidents serve us as inspirations, and they also serve us as warnings. They provide bad examples as well as good. The nation, the Supreme Court has said, has "no right to expect that it will always have wise and humane rulers, sincerely attached to the principles of the Constitution. Wicked men, ambitious of power, with hatred of liberty and contempt of law, may fill the place once occupied by Washington and Lincoln."

The men in the White House express the ideals and the values, the frailties and the flaws, of the voters who send them there. It is altogether natural that we should want to know more about the virtues and the vices of the fellows we have elected to govern us. As we know more about them, we will know more about ourselves. The French political philosopher Joseph de Maistre said, "Every nation has the government it deserves."

At the start of the twenty-first century, forty-two men have made it to the Oval Office. (George W. Bush is counted our forty-third president, because Grover Cleveland, who served nonconsecutive terms, is counted twice.) Of the parade of presidents, a dozen or so lead the polls periodically conducted by historians and political scientists. What makes a great president?

Great presidents possess, or are possessed by, a vision of an ideal America. Their passion, as they grasp the helm, is to set the ship of state on the right course toward the port they seek. Great presidents also have a deep psychic connection with the needs, anxieties, dreams of people. "I do not believe," said Wilson, "that any man can lead who does not act . . . under the impulse of a profound sympathy with those whom he leads—a sympathy which is insight—an insight which is of the heart rather than of the intellect."

"All of our great presidents," said Franklin D. Roosevelt, "were leaders of thought at a time when certain ideas in the life of the nation had to be clarified." So Washington incarnated the idea of federal union, Jefferson and Jackson the idea of democracy, Lincoln union and freedom, Cleveland rugged honesty. Theodore Roosevelt and Wilson, said FDR, were both "moral leaders, each in his own way and his own time, who used the presidency as a pulpit."

To succeed, presidents not only must have a port to seek but they must convince Congress and the electorate that it is a port worth seeking. Politics in a democracy is ultimately an educational process, an adventure in persuasion and consent. Every president stands in Theodore Roosevelt's bully pulpit.

The greatest presidents in the scholars' rankings, Washington, Lincoln, and Franklin Roosevelt, were leaders who confronted and overcame the republic's greatest crises. Crisis widens presidential opportunities for bold and imaginative action. But it does not guarantee presidential greatness. The crisis of secession did not spur Buchanan or the crisis of depression spur Hoover to creative leadership. Their inadequacies in the face of crisis allowed Lincoln and the second Roosevelt to show the difference individuals make to history. Still, even in the absence of first-order crisis, forceful and persuasive presidents—Jackson, Jefferson, Theodore Roosevelt, Ronald Reagan—are able to impose their own priorities on the country.

The diverse drama of the presidency offers a fascinating set of tales. Biographies of American presidents constitute a chronicle of wisdom and folly, nobility and pettiness, courage and cunning, forthrightness and deceit, quarrel and consensus. The turmoil perennially swirling around the White House illuminates the heart of the American democracy.

It is the aim of the American Presidents series to present the grand panorama of our chief executives in volumes compact enough for the busy reader, lucid enough for the student, authoritative enough for the scholar. Each volume offers a distillation of character and career. I hope that these lives will give readers some understanding of the pitfalls and potentialities of the presidency and also of the responsibilities of citizenship. Truman's famous sign—"The buck stops here"—tells only half the story. Citizens cannot escape the ultimate responsibility. It is in the voting booth, not on the presidential desk, that the buck finally stops.

—Arthur M. Schlesinger, Jr.

Prologue

Good Lord! What is VAN!—for though simple he looks,
Tis a task to unravel his looks and his crooks;
With his depths and his shallows, his good and his evil,
All in all, he's a Riddle *must puzzle the devil.*

—DAVY CROCKETT, *The Life of Martin Van Buren* (1835)

In June 1854, a small, elderly man rented rooms overlooking the central plaza of Sorrento, the ancient city jutting into the Mediterranean from a peninsula south of Naples. In a place originally devoted to the worship of the Sirens, the women who drove seafarers mad with their blandishments, he had come to hear the muse of history, and to write the story of his life.

To the locals, of course, he was merely another paying customer. They could not be expected to know that their guest was the eighth president of the United States, Martin Van Buren—by far the eldest living president, and the last of the great generation of leaders who had held the stage during the turbulent period between the War of 1812 and the Mexican War. Jackson, Adams, Clay, Webster, Calhoun—all dead—and still Van Buren soldiered on, besting his adversaries yet again by the simple fact of his endurance. "At the age of seventy-one, and in a foreign land, I commence a sketch of the principal events of my life," he wrote with a faintly triumphal air.

In truth, there was something less than presidential in his appearance, and the people of Sorrento might be forgiven for their indifference. At five feet six inches, Van Buren was the shortest American leader since James Madison. He now looked older than his pictures, which included some of the first daguerreotypes taken of a former president, and the thin wisps of hair around his scalp gave him a mild, cherubic appearance. Long ago, in compensation for his baldness, he had grown a pair of truly executive sideburns, to use a term that would not come into vogue until an inept Civil War general, Ambrose E. Burnside, gave it currency. But southern Italy was still a hodgepodge of small kingdoms and provincial concerns, one of many parts of the globe where the creation of the world's first democracy had made absolutely no difference to anyone. If Van Buren's sideburns were worthy of an Augustus, still it was unclear to the people watching him who, exactly, he was. That problem has not entirely disappeared.

As Van Buren addressed himself to the task of self-definition, he reflected on his nearness to Pompeii, discovered in 1748 and then being excavated. There the past had come arrestingly to life, thanks to the lava and ash that had swallowed an entire village and captured unbearably ordinary moments for eternity.

Van Buren, too, wanted to preserve a moment frozen in fire. But which volcanic eruption to choose from? His stormy first campaigns? His presidency? The financial catastrophe that ruined it? His rise at an extraordinarily young age to complete political mastery of New York, the most populous state in the Union? Or perhaps none of the above—maybe it was better just to begin with his carefree youth in the Hudson Valley, when the United States of America was less than a decade old, a mere velleity, a gleam in George Washington's eye.

So much had happened since his first campaign, the Revolution of 1800. A stripling of seventeen, he had worked desperately hard for his idols, Jefferson and Burr, and was rewarded with a trip to his first party caucus in Troy, a well-named place to begin the Homeric odyssey that had brought him to the Mediterranean. The epic battles that followed had seemed so intense at the time—the struggle over Missouri, then the tariff, then the bank, then Texas and Mexico, then the bitter Free Soil campaign of 1848, each fight leading to the next, and beneath almost all of them, a secret underlying obsession with the subject that dared not speak its name—slavery. Now they were just historical episodes, already enshrouded in the mist that was creeping over all of his recollections. Before long, they would simply be chapters in a book.

What did it all matter here in Sorrento, where the ghosts of imperial Rome held sway, and two thousand years held about as much significance as the gesticulations of an impatient waiter? Washington, D.C., where he had passed so much of his public life, had once aspired to surpass Rome—ridiculously, a dirty creek was called the Tiber, but of course the name failed to stick. Quite a few of the founders' lofty aspirations now seemed overly ambitious.

As he surveyed the sweep of his life, Van Buren's thoughts must have turned to one of his most meaningful friendships, with the writer Washington Irving. They had met decades ago, and had even become roommates in London in 1831, when Van Buren was expecting to become the American envoy, before a rival's treachery did him in. But it went much deeper than that. In 1809, Irving had lived in Van Buren's native Kinderhook while he was recovering from the death of his fiancée and searching out Hudson Valley ghost stories for material. In fact, he lived in the same house that Van Buren would later christen Lindenwald ("Linden forest") when he acquired it as his country seat. While inhabiting Van Buren's future home, Irving created some of the most enduring characters in American literature, including Ichabod Crane and Diedrich Knickerbocker. But no story better illustrates the tension between the American past and present than "Rip Van Winkle," Irving's masterpiece and a parable for the frustrated historian, out of sorts with current events, and unable to arrange the past exactly as he would like it. As the former president assembled the fragmented pieces of his life, stretching back to the earliest years of the republic, he must have felt like a disoriented Rip Van Buren, the creature of distant time and place.

But we will never know the answer to these speculations, because with characteristic opaqueness, Van Buren never wrote the book that would have revealed himself to us. Yes, his autobiography is arguably the first presidential memoir, and for that reason alone it holds real interest. But it stops short of the presidency, digresses like a runaway train, and reveals only the skimpiest personal information. There are flashes of personality here and there, and glimpses of the greatness he both encountered and summoned in his long career, but these moments are obfuscated by the long, stem-winding passages that constitute the core of the Van Buren opus. If possible, it is even harder to slog through than the memoirs of Herbert Hoover, Dwight D. Eisenhower, and Harry Truman, and that is saying something.

That is only one of the reasons that Martin Van Buren eludes us today. He has been escaping pursuers since they began chasing him, which may explain why "the Fox" was one of his many nicknames. Has any other president held so many? The Red Fox of Kinderhook. The Little Magician. The Enchanter. The Careful Dutchman. The Great Manager. The Master Spirit. The American Talleyrand. King Martin. Matty Van.

This surfeit of sobriquets suggests both a familiarity with Van Buren and an ultimate failure to catch him. The names cancel each other out, they disagree with each other, and they suggest an inscrutability that still hangs like Spanish moss around him. Truly, there was something vulpine about the Fox. He eludes easy classification by the phrenologists of the historical profession, who measure the bumps and gouges of presidents to determine their lasting significance (at last glance, he ranked twenty-first out of forty-three). He eludes us because he apparently destroyed those parts of his correspondence that would have revealed his innermost secrets.

He eludes us because his loyal confederates divulged precious little of their private thinking about him.

But mostly he eludes us because no one is looking for him anymore. He's a lost president, floating in purgatory between Jackson and the Civil War, unremembered by most, and doomed to occupy the least heroic categories designed by historians (he has a lock on "average"). Weirdly, he was placed on a pedestal by Ezra Pound, the architect of lost causes. But that's hardly a case for immortality in our amnesiac culture. On the extremely rare occasions when his image is presented before modern Americans, it is either disappointing (the cad-president in *Amistad* who turns a deaf ear to the African plea for freedom) or farcical (on *Seinfeld*, the idol of a secret society in New York, "the Van Buren Boys," whom Kramer discovers when he accidentally sticks eight fingers in the air—the invocation for all loyalists to the eighth president).

Once it was not so. Approximately six generations ago, it was impossible not to have an opinion about Martin Van Buren. And these opinions were not for the faint of heart. In certain quarters, Van Buren was the most hated man in America. He was pilloried in cartoons (where his size and baldness made him an easy target), attacked in speeches on the floor of Congress, and privately despised by millions. At the same time, he was defended by his stalwart friends, and admired, if not exactly loved, by millions more—particularly the small freeholders who felt threatened by the incursions of new elites—callous bankers, wanton plantation owners, greedy merchants and factory owners. He was accused of being noncommittal (a word he is said to have invented), but in truth it was America that had trouble making up its mind about him. For good or ill, he provided a steady stream of fodder for the new penny newspapers flooding eastern cities, and his every utterance was subjected to close scrutiny by hierophants of America's political religion. Why did so many people find humor in the name Little Van? Because he was big. It was the pictures that got small.

There was a widespread refusal, then as now, to admit that Martin Van Buren accomplished what he did. In what might have been the most talented political generation in American history, he alone achieved what every politician in America wanted desperately: the succession of Andrew Jackson. Has there ever been a rival to the class of 1782? That year saw the birth of Daniel Webster, John C. Calhoun, Thomas Hart Benton, and Martin Van Buren. Each rose to dominate his state, and then battled the others in the Senate. Only one became president.

When he was elected in 1836, Van Buren became the first chief executive from New York, and the first ethnic president. Both facts are important. New York City, with two hundred thousand people in 1830, and many more in 1836, was indisputably the capital of the American future. The Erie Canal, finished in 1825, had brought the enormous riches of the interior into New York's backyard. The city was growing exponentially in all directions. From Ireland, from Germany, from a thousand little villages in New England, Ohio, and Pennsylvania, young men and women were streaming into Manhattan to write a better future for themselves. They were not exactly Jefferson's rural yeomanry; in fact, they represented a deep threat to his stubborn vision of an Anglo-Saxon agricultural republic. (Jefferson felt, with pathological intensity, that cities were an open sore on the body politic.) They were an unruly lot, living in cramped quarters, working desperately hard for a living that no one was about to give them. But they were good Americans, and deserved a voice in the affairs of the republic. Martin Van Buren helped to give it to them.

Van Buren was also our first president (and our last, save Kennedy) without a trace of Anglo-Saxon bloodlines. In our putative nation of nations, every other president has come from an English-speaking household, and rather high English at that. Van Buren grew up speaking Dutch, a relic of the time before the Revolution when the inland waterways of North America were a polyglot blend of non-Anglophone communities. His family had resisted intermarriage with Yankees for five generations, and Van Buren trumpeted the fact proudly in his autobiography. In fact, the clannish Van Burens had married each other to avoid diluting the mix. He would seem a little foreign all his life.

But it is perhaps unwise to focus exclusively on the presidency, as Van Buren and so many of his rivals did. Yes, that is the reason this book is being written—because Van Buren happened to occupy the Executive Mansion between 1837 and 1841, and therefore earned a place in this series. But his lasting importance lies elsewhere, in his contribution to the delicate and sometimes not-so-delicate machinery of the American political system. Between the Revolution that created our nation and the Civil War that tested and strengthened it, an elaborate mechanism was created to put the theoretical ideas of the founders into everyday, working practice. It involved some obvious steps forward, such as enlarging the suffrage (between 1824 and 1840, the bookends of Van Buren's federal career, the number of voters increased from 400,000 to 2.4 million). And it involved old-fashioned, brutal political warfare, including the creation of a new party and the application of political muscle to ensure the party's survival.

More than any other American, Van Buren helped to create this new democratic mechanism. In varying degrees, he shaped the invention of the party caucus, the nominating convention, the patronage system, the publicity network, and the Democratic Party itself. When the party came into existence in the mid-1820s, it signaled a radical departure from American history to that point. The founders had deplored the idea of "faction," and Jefferson had tried to cloak his counterinsurgency as a return to original principles. With Van Buren, it was different—the party was celebrated as a legitimate end in itself. More than just any end, it grew into a disciplined organization to rival any corporation in America. More than just an organization, it was a movement, perhaps even a religion.

Van Buren was the general manager and apostle of this unprecedented entity. He spoke a new dialect for the new men of the nineteenth century, a dialect that had not yet been spoken in America, but which has been spoken at a loud volume ever since. For his boldness, he earned the contempt of his enemies, most of whom still believed in a world where landowning gentry controlled the destinies of their dependents, and opposition was tantamount to disobedience. Now and then, he earned their contempt, for he played the game of politics with as much ferocity as any of his rivals. But he deserves our grudging respect for his vision of a modern political system that allowed democracy to grow beyond the founding documents into something tangible for millions of disenfranchised Americans.

Van Buren lacked Webster's eloquence, or Calhoun's fire, or Benton's physical presence, but his political vision exceeded anyone's of his generation. He saw the shifting demographics that were ultimately going to give the urban North more power than the plantation South. He saw that New York, as it gained electoral strength, would no longer need to take a backseat to the squires of Virginia, who viewed the White House as yet another plantation along the Potomac. He saw the emptiness of the temporary alliances that dominated politics during the so-called Era of Good Feelings, and perceived the need for a great party, built around a New York–Virginia axis, but open to restless young men from all regions, that would harness their energy and transform American politics forever.

The idea was borrowed from his two mentors, Thomas Jefferson and Aaron Burr, who had joined forces in 1800, but Van Buren was able to build a far more enduring alliance than the fusion of two combustible elements like Burr and Jefferson would ever achieve. Van Buren's North-South base, drawing on well-run state operations with like-minded operators, was not so different from the model that would be built a century later by his distant kinsman and fellow Knickerbocker Franklin Roosevelt. He used it to win the presidency, and then, in one of those reversals that periodically turn American politics into Greek tragedy, he nearly destroyed what he had built with the first major third-party campaign in American history, the Free Soil movement of 1848. In that quixotic effort, he resembled no one so much as his other presidential kinsman Theodore Roosevelt. He did all that, and he helped to popularize the most useful word in world history, if indeed it is a word: OK. Can any president claim a more pervasive legacy?

It is still hard for us to believe, as it was for his contemporaries. There was something in Van Buren's appearance that struck observers as vaguely wrong. It was not merely that he was short and bald, or that he grew those foppish sideburns that seemed to widen his body by several inches in the wrong direction. Something in his very being enraged his enemies, and he was never able to persuade them that he was the legitimate heir to Jackson, even after he had won the White House. They savaged him with burlesques and cartoons and speeches on the floor of Congress, hinting that he wore a corset and drawing dark inferences about the Madeira he drank and the fine china he ordered for state dinners. It was widely whispered that he was the bastard progeny of Aaron Burr—a terrible slur in 1827, the year that John Quincy Adams rapturously wrote the gossip in his diary.

All this innuendo was even more unlikely given the relative poverty of Van Buren's upbringing—an indigence exceeded only by Jackson and Lincoln among the early presidents, and not matched by too many since. He is one of only two men elected president without the benefit of military service or a college education (Grover Cleveland is the other). But his humble background was one of the reasons his enemies disdained him, while also attacking the urbane tastes he had cultivated to mask his modest origin. With some enemies, you just can't win. Like almost every Democratic president since then, his enjoyment of life was twisted by his critics into hypocrisy and selfishness, and proof that his form of democracy was insincere—the bulk of the criticism coming, of course, from the most abject defenders of the status quo.

Not all his shortcomings were exaggerated. Some were even underappreciated. Like every politician in the antebellum, he failed to confront the ticking time bomb of slavery. Or to be more specific, he neglected it when he could have done something, ahead of the pack, and turned to it only late in his career, with mixed results. Slavery was not just a moral crisis; it was a political problem of the highest magnitude, and as a clairvoyant party boss he should have seen it coming. But the fact that Southerners thought him pro-northern and Northerners thought him pro-southern conveys something of the delicacy of his predicament. It is true, as Dante wrote, that the hottest circles of hell are reserved for those who, in a time of crisis, preserve their neutrality. But to have been braver and wiser in 1837 would almost certainly have doomed him to political irrelevance. The nation was not yet ready—not even close (part of Lincoln's genius is that he arrived at a moment when it was possible to become Lincoln). Like most Jacksonians, Van Buren tilted at windmills and lunged at chimeras, consumed by the "monster" of the Bank while ignoring the genuine monster nursing at America's bosom.

It is also true that he was ambitious and calculating. Are there any presidents who were not? Jefferson? Please. Lincoln? TR? FDR? You must be joking. Van Buren did hire cronies, as all presidents have, and fired more of his rivals' appointees than was customary at the time. He could be a ruthless infighter. At his best, the Little Magician turned opponents into chumps and made problems vanish into his hat. People like that kind of magic. But was it magic? Or just effective politics, conducted by a virtuoso ahead of his time, using twentieth-century hardball while most of his contemporaries were still playing rounders? In his epic biography of LBJ, a shark whom Van Buren resembles in some respects (though certainly not the physical), Robert Caro discusses the lesser political arts that matter behind the scene—vote counting, deal making, favorable and unfavorable publicity at just the right moment. Like Johnson, Van Buren understood these pressure points instinctively. It is not the stuff of Young Reader Biographies of Great Americans, but it is, for better or worse, how America works.

His mastery of these invisible skills may explain why so much power seemed to flow to him, without apparent exertion. The caustic Virginian John Randolph of Roanoke wrote that he "rowed to his object with muffled oars." Time after time, his opponents sensed his presence at the levers of the mechanism, throwing switches and adjusting gear ratios to make the system hum. They never understood how he had arrived at his knowledge so effortlessly, without the blustery speeches and rodomontades that defined political fame for those living in the eighteenth century, as so many Americans still were in the early republic. Van Buren resembled one of Nathaniel Hawthorne's fictitious scientists—Ethan Brand or Roger Chillingsworth—who mysteriously acquire a forbidden knowledge of the dark arts, emblematic of the great industrial changes altering Puritan New England forever. A little magician, indeed.

But many of the charges against Van Buren were unfounded. One of the most serious is that he refused to take a stand on the issues, that he was too "Van Burenish," to use an adjective of the day. He rather enjoyed the reputation—in his autobiography, he relished the story of two men who heard him speak on the tariff and afterward praised him profusely for his eloquent argument. After a brief pause, one of them then asked him sheepishly which side of the great question his speech had defended.

After examining the evidence, I find no reason to believe that he failed to speak and act on important problems. He did, over and over again. Not always in the way that we would like him to, from our pitch-perfect perspective. But still, he made hard decisions, and he generally made them well. From early adulthood onward, he made a series of brave commitments to the cause of democracy, both in his legal career defending small tenants against the great landlords of the Hudson Valley and in politics. Each time, he was severely rebuked by the wealthy patrons who tried to enlist him in their narrow causes. Each time, he overcame the insults and outdistanced his would-be protectors, which enraged them all the more. One of his most courageous decisions was his refusal to join the stampede for admitting Texas, with all of its slave territory, into the union. It cost him the presidency and he knew it, but he stuck to his guns.

I want in this book to bring Martin Van Buren back from the dead, because he is important. In so doing, I want to steer a middle course between the partisans who tried to lift Van Buren's pudgy frame into the pantheon—an effort that collapsed under the weight of its absurdity—and his legions of character assassins, who wanted the world to see him through their inverted binoculars. After a century and a half of neglect, Van Buren deserves some attention, and some accuracy as well.

In so doing, I want to show how much effort and emotion is invested in any presidency—not merely the gargantuan political struggles that lead to and then undo an administration, but the simple life of the republic over any four years in our history. I want to show how much of American history belongs to people whose names we cannot remember—not just Van Buren, but the tens of thousands of nameless coopers and cordwainers and field hands who spoke through him, in all of their languages.

It is easy to minimize the importance of a single-term presidency, especially when that term contains a disaster. Let's face it, depression presidents are, for lack of a better word, depressing. Like Herbert Hoover, like George H. W. Bush, like James Buchanan, Van Buren had the bad luck to be a one-term president in punishing times. The Panic of 1837 was the worst economic crisis to date in American history. It sent shudders around the world, proving how global the American economy had already become.

But that does not mean those four years were insignificant. On the contrary, something essential happened between 1837 and 1841. It was a hinge of history—one of those moments when a door latch silently clicks open and the mood of a nation changes ineffably. Virginia Woolf wrote, "on or about December 1910, human character changed." For all its frustration, Van Buren's tenure was no less pivotal.

How rich those depression years were! Americans were caught vertiginously between the feeling that something was ending and something very new was beginning. The oldest of the revolutionaries were dying off—James Madison in June 1836 (six days short of the fourth of July—a pity), Aaron Burr in September of the same year, on the eve of seeing his protégé elected. Sally Hemings had died a year earlier, though few noticed. In the late 1830s, the body of George Washington was removed from its coffin and placed in a marble sarcophagus, and this macabre newspaper account reveals how intensely dependent Americans still were on the revolutionary past that was slipping from their fingers:

GENERAL WASHINGTON.—The remains of this illustrious man, the Father and Saviour of his country, were recently placed in the sarcophagus made by Mr. Struthers of this city, from whom we learn that, when the vault and coffin were opened 'where they had lain him,' the sacred form of Washington was discovered in a wonderful state of preservation. The high pale brow wore a calm and serene expression; and the lips, pressed still together, had a grave and solemn smile, such as they doubtless wore when the first president gave up his mortal life for an immortal existence; 'When his soft breath, with pain, was yielded to the elements again.' The impressive aspect of the great departed overpowered the man whose lot it was to transfer the hallowed dust to its last tenement, and he was unable to conceal his emotions. He placed his hand upon the ample forehead, once highest in the ranks of battle, or throbbing with the cares of the infant empire, and he lamented, we doubt not, that the voice of fame could not provoke that silent clay to life again, or pour its tones of revival into the dull cold ear of death.

But the times were startlingly modern as well. What wasn't invented in the 1830s? The railroad hurtled through American lives at sickening speeds up to thirty miles an hour, and tracks spread like spiderwebs across the landscape (the United States boasted 2,816 miles of tracks in 1840, up from 23 in 1830, and well ahead of Britain's 1,331 miles). The first daguerreotypes captured light and reality as no painter ever could (the earliest American example, from September 1839, showed a blurry church near Washington Square in New York). Samuel Morse, one of the first American photographers, was getting ready to unveil his new telegraph. Charles Goodyear stumbled across the formula for vulcanized rubber, perhaps winning World War II for the Allies by doing so. The Hoe type revolutionized the printed word, leading to the mass printing of newspapers and the creation of modern journalism. The list goes on and on. It was, in short, the birth of modernity. John D. Rockefeller, born in Richford, New York, on July 8, 1839, lived until 1937, within the lifetime of Elvis Presley.

An extraordinary number of foreign travelers visited America in the 1830s, sensing that the future of the world was being enacted here. Tocqueville's books came out in 1835 and 1840; he was followed by scores of imitators from across Europe, but especially from England, now waking up to the brawn of its bastard stepchild. Americans, too, caught the fever. In 1837, Ralph Waldo Emerson stood up and announced that America no longer needed Europe; his speech was called America's declaration of literary independence. At nearly the same moment, young men across the land aggressively claimed their destinies. In Springfield, Illinois, Abraham Lincoln gave his first major speech, announcing that one generation had passed and it was time for a new generation to take charge. In Hudson, Ohio, John Brown experienced an epiphany and stood up in the back of a prayer meeting to announce that he was ready to destroy slavery by any means necessary. In Baltimore, a young slave named Frederick Bailey formed a secret debating club, the East Baltimore Mental Improvement Society, to debate the ethics of bondage with a circle of white friends—a step toward his escape a year later and his reinvention as Frederick Douglass.

As these young Americans found themselves, the nation swelled with the daily arrival of ever-growing numbers of immigrants, perhaps moved by the grand talk about freedom, but more likely just looking for a home. The 1840 census showed that Thomas Jefferson's simple agrarian republic now had almost 17 million people. New York City alone had three hundred thousand people. That figure would give Calhoun nightmares—Calhoun who had resisted the rise of Van Buren since he first came to Washington, hoping to perpetuate his sinister vision of a slave-based republic, and now helpless before the onslaught of humanity coming across the Atlantic, to Van Buren's North. Their rivalry, containing the seeds of the internecine conflict to come, bears more scrutiny than historians have accorded it.

It is perhaps this aspect of the four years that is most noteworthy. Between 1837 and 1841, it became clear to sentient observers that an apocalyptic battle was looming between North and South; or, more accurately, between Union and Slavery—a struggle that would dwarf the acrimonious debates over economic policy that had dominated the previous decade. The shelves of New England libraries bulge with tracts from the late 1830s attacking the peculiar institution. The South was equally recalcitrant, passing a gag rule in the House that prevented any resolutions treating the subject of slavery—an outrageous violation of free speech. The storm was still two decades off, but its headwinds were already blowing fiercely.

These were hard facts for Americans to accept. They were then, as now, deeply patriotic about their past, and perhaps even more so about their future. There was a mania for new utopian schemes, from religious revivalism to bizarre cults like the followers of Sylvester Graham, who believed that cold showers, hard mattresses, a diet of rough fiber (he invented the graham cracker), and abstention from sex would lead to a healthy life and afterlife. Graham was once nearly drawn and quartered by a mob of butchers in Boston after complaining that raw meat, if looked at the right way, could arouse impure thoughts.

Between 1837 and 1841, Americans encountered three important reality checks that suddenly made the future less appetizing. The Panic of 1837 taught that capitalism was fallible. The Log Cabin campaign of 1840, with its false promises and hard cider entreaties, taught that democracy was fallible. And rising rage over slavery taught that the Union itself was fallible. After years of thinking that they were uniquely virtuous and that God had smiled on the American republic (the perfectly scripted Fourth of July exits of Jefferson and Adams proved it), Americans had some real problems on their hands.

In other words, Van Buren had his work cut out for him as president. It would take an extremely imaginative biographer to claim that he succeeded; it is less Van Burenish to call his presidency a disaster and leave it at that. But I would like to suggest that it was a more interesting disaster than most. His failures showed how difficult it was to assemble a democratic coalition in the face of withering pressure from economic chaos, regional discord, and the conservative enemies who never gave him a moment's peace. His successes, rare though they were, showed an evolving sense of government's role in strengthening what Van Buren called "the Democracy"—not just the party, but the entire people (at least the people who were not female, African, or Native American). All told, his turmoil deepens our astonishment that the tiny government created by a small cluster of gentlemen in Philadelphia in

1787 not only survived intact, but grew into the most powerful human force on earth.

It certainly was not written on a stone tablet that things were going to turn out this way. In fact, when Van Buren died after a long tenure as ex-president (the fifth-longest after Herbert Hoover, Gerald Ford, John Adams, and Jimmy Carter), the future could not have looked darker. Van Buren, a child of the Revolution, expired on July 24, 1862, with no sign that the end of the war was in sight, his party and country in tatters.

But perhaps he did not despair. He had faced adversity over and over again, and survived everything that life and politics threw at him. His sunny disposition never faltered, at least not in public. He knew a crucial American fact, one that still drives Europeans crazy: optimism breeds optimism, and relentless good cheer, even when artificial, can turn a rout into a strategic retreat. He may have known that, in the very month he died, Abraham Lincoln signed the Morrill Act (laying the foundation for our great state universities), the Pacific Railroad Act, and presented the first draft of the Emancipation Proclamation to his cabinet. That fundamental belief in the future—so bold as to almost constitute effrontery—would have warmed Van Buren's heart.

Martin Van Buren had always cared about the future—he boasted in his inaugural that he was the first president born after independence, and insisted that "I belong to a later age." In certain ways, he had brought the future into existence, removing the old-fashioned politicians who failed to get it and helping America grow from infancy into something like adolescence—a perfect word to convey the turbulent mood swings, lingering pustules of animosity, and general bad hair of the Van Buren era.

He deserves to be reconnected to that future—to us. Not falsely praised—he would not want that. Well, all right, he would. Rather, Van Buren's life should be honestly reexamined for the truths of his own time and ours. A grand total of six American communities were named after him, presumably during his brief moment in the sun, in Arkansas, Indiana, Kentucky, Maine, Missouri, and Ohio. Their combined population adds up to about ten thousand people, far more than have ever read a book about him. After all that he lived through, he deserves more. Perhaps this profile will begin the process of explaining him more fully, expanding upon the effort he began alongside the Mediterranean, with the Sirens singing their entreaties and Clio whispering in his ear.

1

Kinderhook

Legend has it that Martin Van Buren was once received at a royal reception by Queen Adelaide of the Netherlands. Before a crowd of courtiers and swells, she politely asked the distinguished Dutch-American how far back he could trace his ancestry. Van Buren bowed deeply and responded, "As far back as Kinderhook, Your Majesty." That was vintage Van Buren, saying everything and nothing at once.

To begin to peel back Van Buren's mysteries, there is no more logical place to start than his hometown. Kinderhook is located in Columbia County, New York, on the east bank of the Hudson, twenty miles south of Albany. Like all hometowns, it is far more than a destination to be casually entered into a Yahoo! search engine. For Van Buren, it was the opposite of a terminus—it was a place of origin, and for most of his forebears, the sum and circumference of geographical knowledge. In other words, it was a place to be left behind.

Today's Kinderhook is a charming village, eager to promote its link to the Dutch past and to its two celebrities, Van Buren and Washington Irving. It boasts the usual saintly relics associated with medieval pilgrimages, including Van Buren's fine china toilet, one of the first such contrivances installed in a private residence in the

United States, and its curio shops and bed-and-breakfasts ooze quaintness. To be sure, it is as lovely a place to escape to as from. Like other small seats of presidential aspiration—say, Plymouth, Vermont (pop. 440), or West Branch, Iowa (pop. 1,908), or Plains, Georgia (pop. 716)—it inspires with the notion that anyone from anywhere can become the leader of the world's most powerful nation.

But there is more to Kinderhook (pop. 1,293) than just careful scenery. Like all old towns in the postindustrial North, it has tired neighborhoods at the periphery, marginal in every sense. The Salvation Army is doing a thriving business, as are a couple of auto body shops, the Shear Magic Hair Salon, and an Off-Track Betting facility. Along the highways leading in and out of town are the careworn signs of roadside capitalism we routinely drive by without much noticing: AKC BEAGLES 4 SALE, or, even more economically, BAIT. The would-be Irving, eager to paint Kinderhook as an eighteenth-century Dutch movie set, does so at his peril. Real people live here.

In fact, Kinderhook's quaintness was earned the hard way. Throughout its early history, it witnessed one political struggle after another, usually pitting the landed gentry whose mansions dot the upper Hudson like so many navigational beacons against the regular folks who also happened to live here. More than most towns on the upper Hudson, Kinderhook emerged as an island of two-party democracy in a region that was at that time anything but democratic. The first clue to its identity lies in its location at a desirable wide spot on the Hudson, where a creek flows in from the east. Local histories claim that this was the place where Henry Hudson, after traveling across the Atlantic and up the great river, decided he'd seen enough of America and turned the *Half Moon* around, headed for home. Writing of Hudson's U-turn, a wordy antiquarian called Kinderhook "the Ultima Thule of his personal explorations and the Ne Plus Ultra of his desires." That is too poetic for most stomachs, but it comes as no surprise to learn that the favorable location soon turned into a bustling little port, and that its numbers grew as the Dutch poured into the Hudson Valley in the seventeenth century.

But like any real estate story, the key to Kinderhook's story is location (there is still a Van Buren Realty at the center of town). This precise spot was one of the few places on the upper Hudson that fell outside the great manorial tracts given to the great patroons—the enormously wealthy seventeenth-century landholders who controlled giant tracts of land as if they were feudal lords, which they were. Paradoxically, the Hudson Valley, future home to stalwart Democrats like Van Buren and FDR, was one of the least democratic regions in colonial America. The mighty Van Rensselaers owned a sprawling entity known as Rensselaerswyck, three-quarters of a million acres in Columbia, Albany, and Rensselaer counties; the equally baronial Livingstons claimed 250,000 acres in Columbia County.

Yet Americans have a way of overpowering—or, better yet, ignoring—the moldy parchments written in secret chambers in Europe. The settlers who came to Kinderhook had little patience for these claims, some of which exceeded the size of entire European nations, and all of which were vague and difficult to enforce. As a result, this particular zone of democracy along the Hudson attracted numerous citizens who prized freedom from authority. Soon, roads were linking this favored spot to the other clusters of semi-Americans living in the region. "The Great New England Path" had once brought Native Americans from Massachusetts, and grew into an important colonial highway connecting Kinderhook to Albany in one direction and Boston and New York in the other.

Naturally, these axial roads drew travelers, lawyers, and other miscreants populating the eighteenth-century landscape. The pace quickened in the aftermath of the French and Indian War, which had opened up vast reaches of New York's hinterland, and the American Revolution, which did more of the same. Travelers streamed over the highway from the east, eager to start something better in the new world that always lay just over the horizon. Many tarried for a night or two in a modest tavern run by the easygoing Abraham Van Buren. And it was here, on December 5, 1782, that Martin Van Buren entered the world, literally born to the bosom of politics, for his father's tavern doubled as the local polling place at election time.

At first, there was precious little to indicate that the infant would merit the future interest of historians. The first Van Burens had slouched toward Kinderhook in 1631 after a long journey from Holland. The progenitor, Cornelis, did not even have a proper last name, so his son Marten added the Van Buren (being thousands of miles from the old country made a distinguished lineage that much easier to fabricate). They were joined by neighbors and cousins— more or less one and the same—and discovered an early form of the American Dream, defined as agriculture and the creation of more Van Burens. If the myth is that Americans are always on the move, always improving themselves, there was little in the Van Buren saga to support it. For a century and a half, they stayed exactly where they were—close to the land and close to each other. Like characters in a Gabriel García Márquez novel, they regenerated themselves across the centuries, oblivious to the upheavals happening around them. Kinderhook was as inbred as any island, and more than a few Van Burens married their kin, including Van Buren's father and grandfather. In his autobiography, the future president boasted with a Bosnian insularity: "My family was from Holland, without a single intermarriage with one of different extraction from the time of the arrival of the first emigrant to that of the marriage of my eldest son, embracing a period of over two centuries and including six generations."

You can get a pretty good idea of life in old Kinderhook by looking at any Dutch genre painting of the seventeenth century— families sitting around the hearth, cows lowing in the fields, young men and women flirting in the shadows. It was a world that Vermeer would have instantly recognized—the sleepy town rising and setting with the sun, and following the same harvest rhythms of any farm community. Authority flowed lazily downward from the local gentry, like a mountain stream. Information was spread through conversation and eavesdropping, and outsiders were distrusted. In the 1780s, after some farm animals disappeared, a local rumor blamed a wild, mixed-race family of blacks, whites, and Indians, all named Johnston, who allegedly lived in little huts in the Pine Woods outside of town, and allowed illicit relations between brother and sister. Like their neighbors, the Van Burens—all seven families with that name—spoke furtively in Dutch to one another, attended the Dutch Reformed Church, and prayed to a Dutch God. Those who were not Van Burens were more than likely to be Van Alens, Van Nesses, or Van Schaacks. Washington Irving was captivated by these aspects of Kinderhook during his stay there, and in turn captured some of it in his writing—the low-roofed dwelling, the spreading sycamore, the henpecked husband sneaking out of earshot for a dram.

In many ways, Abraham Van Buren was the embodiment of an Irving character—a bit careless about money, and not the most eager young man to settle down with a wife. In fact, he was thirty-nine by the time that he surrendered his independence in, of all years, 1776. That year he married Maria Hoes Van Alen, a widow with three children. There is some evidence that she completes the Irving profile as a sturdy, self-reliant housewife, not one to suffer fools gladly, although in truth very little is known about this crucial formative influence on the future president. She bore two more children to Van Buren before Martin was born, five days before a provisional treaty was signed ending the war. Three more children would follow, giving Martin eight siblings, spread out evenly around him. It was a middling debut in every sense.

The Van Burens belonged utterly to the social organism of Kinderhook, and yet their status in the hierarchy was mediocre at best. Like a quarter of Kinderhookers, Abraham owned slaves—six of them. This was not as unusual as it sounds (New York would not abolish slavery until 1827) but still, the fact does not square easily with Van Buren's future as a defender of small freeholds. Yet this was no tidewater mansion. The one-and-a-half-story wooden tavern housed not only its paying customers, but the sixteen Van Buren dependents, white and black. How the occupants of this strange multiracial condominium coexisted we can only guess at dimly, and most historians have preferred to remain mute on the subject. There is no evidence that Van Buren, the first and last northern president to know slavery up close, felt either a deep revulsion toward the peculiar institution or the remotest desire to save it. More than anything, it seems that he wanted to leave this overcrowded household, reeking of inefficiency and indigence, in the past where it belonged—and that may be as close to an anti-slavery argument as he ever got.

Clearly, there was a great distance between this crowded household and the manorial dwellings dominating the vast patroonships of the Hudson Valley. Perhaps for this reason, Abraham Van Buren identified with the democratic hopes of the new era.

There is precious little information on either parent in the slender campaign biographies that began to accompany Van Buren's presidential stirrings in the 1830s, but what there is is illuminating. The elder Van Buren was "a whig in the Revolution, an antifederalist in 1788, and an early supporter of Jefferson." There is the hint of something more than indolence in that sentence—a genuine political feeling that was translated from father to son.

In his autobiography, Van Buren reveals just how far removed from the center of Kinderhook his father's little tavern really was. An unfamiliar wounded tone crept in when he remembered the grandees of Columbia County, his awe at their great "reputation and distinction," and his difficulty at proving his worth to a society that was still more democratic in name than in spirit. For all his parents' economies, they struggled for their meager existence. Van

Buren damned his father with faint praise as "an unassuming amiable man . . . utterly devoid of the spirit of accumulation." Worse,
"his property, originally moderate, was gradually reduced until he
could but illy afford to bestow the necessary means upon the education of his children." That tone of anger, from the talented son of
a second marriage, wondering about his place in the world, and surrounded on all sides by oafish conformity, would later fuel suspicions about Van Buren's parentage.

And yet, a tavern was not such a dismal place to grow up for a
young boy with a head for politics. Here the locals aired their grievances and gossip. The mail came, as did travelers bearing important
dispatches between Albany and the city growing recklessly at the
mouth of the Hudson. Political leaders came as well, including
the most charismatic of all New York Republicans, Aaron Burr.
Inevitably, these impressions acted as an incubator on the sensitive
political intelligence growing inside the tavern walls. Like young
Dick Nixon in his father's service station in Whittier, California, or
Jimmy Carter in his father's general store in Plains, or Bill Clinton
in his grandfather's store in a mixed-race part of Hope, Arkansas,
Martin Van Buren absorbed it all.

And what gossip there was in those days! Five years before his
birth, the great battle of Saratoga, just upriver, had brought the
rebels their first important victory. Three years later, in the opposite
direction, the lower Hudson witnessed the excitement over Bene-
dict Arnold's attempt to surrender West Point to Major John André.
When Van Buren was born, George Washington was at Newburgh,
not far from West Point, and the British did not finally evacuate
New York until he was a year old. Van Buren was not only the first
president born in the United States, but the only one born to the
revolution itself.

For all its rustic calm, Kinderhook was anxious before, during,
and after the war. The farmers of Columbia County, historically
dominated by the patroons and their toadies, must have felt no little
sympathy with the leveling winds unleashed by the revolution. An

amusing newspaper account from 1775 reveals that a group of young women, gathered for a quilting bee, tarred and feathered a young man who denounced the cause of liberty in their midst. Aftershocks were felt long after war ended, and Kinderhook was uncomfortably close to the agitation that shook western Massachusetts throughout Shays's Rebellion in 1786–87.

To the west, as well, were sources of insecurity—not only Native Americans, but a huge and poorly defined expanse of new territory that required new forms of administration and attracted all manner of people to pass through Kinderhook on their way to meet the challenge. It is important to convey a sense of New York's vastness in the eighteenth century—already an old state, with six generations of Van Burens, but endlessly renewing itself with an incessant stream of empire-builders seeking their fortune in the hinterland. Like Virginia, it was so large that its contours were barely understood—stretching from the Green Mountains of Vermont, not yet a state, to the Great Lakes and the furthest inland reaches of North American settlement. Western and eastern; urban, rural, and pristine; New York's limitless future lay before it like a clearing in the forest, about to be lined with iron rails.

But if Kinderhook was backward in some senses, it was not entirely isolated either. Its location on the river and the roads meant that the little hub was perfectly situated to harness the tidal wave of energies released by the end of the war. In the same year that Van Buren was born, Congress had adopted a Great Seal with the motto *Novus Ordo Seclorum* (And So Begins a New Order for the Ages). Americans took Congress at its word. They began to build a new country before the ink on the treaties was dry.

Historians tell us that *capital*, both the word and the thing, appeared around 1800 in the upper Hudson Valley, as speculators subsidized new businesses and reaped huge profits for their confidence in others. New enterprises sprang up—near Kinderhook, Yankees from New England created the town of Hudson in 1783, and before long it had a thriving whaling business, hundreds of miles from the Atlantic Ocean! The old, familiar rhythms of agricultural life gave way to a new celerity—new men with new attitudes, less inclined to mumble deferentially before their betters, and eager to enjoy life on their own terms. Time and information were of the essence, so people bought watches and read newspapers. Their energy crackled like electricity along the roads connecting Albany to New York and Boston. Some of it, by extension, found its way into the little tavern.

Van Buren was a quick study. In his own words, he possessed "an uncommonly active mind," and he was sent to the local one-room schoolhouse. But owing to his father's pecuniary embarrassment, he left school at thirteen. An acute consciousness of what he gave up pervades his writing. In his autobiography, he bemoans his lack of reading, and writes, "I am now amazed that with such disadvantages I should have been able to pass through such contests as it has been my lot to encounter with so few discomfitures. Much adroitness was often necessary to avoid appearing in debate until I had been able to make myself master of the subject under discussion." His lifelong insecurity on this point may be one of the reasons he and Andrew Jackson became such close friends, to the surprise of Van Buren's better-educated rivals.

If the decision to leave school cost him something, it also brought him closer to the political world that fascinated him. In 1796 Van Buren left home to begin an apprenticeship with the lawyer Francis Silvester, one of Kinderhook's worthies and, like most of the local gentry, a staunch Federalist. The work was hardly glamorous; in exchange for building a fire every day and sweeping out the office, Van Buren received rudimentary training in the law and a glimpse of life inside the Kinderhook elite.

But several half-remembered anecdotes suggest how long the odds still were against Martin Van Buren. On the first day Van Buren reported to work as an apprentice, according to an old campaign biography, he wore "coarse linen and rough woolens his mother had spun and woven." This garment became dirtier over the course of the day, doubtless because one of his duties was to clean the office, and his employer objected to his unkempt appearance. At the end of his first day, after a lecture on the importance of wearing the right clothing, Van Buren disappeared for two days and came back wearing the same expensive outfit that Silvester was wearing when he chastised him. He would never be accused of a casual attitude toward clothing again.

Van Buren was also under pressure from his employer to join the dominant Federalist Party. Another early biography claims that the Federalists noticed his great ability, and that they soon "feared as well as hated him," specifically because his "eloquence at popular meetings in the cause of public rights" filled them with "terror and dismay." That sounds exaggerated, but still, the ruling party had noticed the young talent in their midst. Most of Kinderhook went Federalist, including Van Buren's older half brother, and it would have been easy for him to follow them.

In 1798, Silvester's father won election as a state senator, and all evening the townsfolk celebrated with songs, cannon fire, and copious toasts. It was a defining moment for the fifteen-year-old apprentice. All evening the Silvesters invited him to join them, and he refused, staying in his room. At length, one of them came and sat on his bed. After a long and heartfelt conversation, Van Buren later recalled, "My course had been settled after much reflection, and could not be changed." His principled stand created bickering and "heart burning" on the part of his master, but he stood his ground. There was nothing noncommittal about it.

The campaign biographies tell us that the story did not end there. In that moment, the vitriolic dislike that followed Van Buren like a miasma began to come into existence: "His character was traduced, his person ridiculed, his principles branded as infamous, his integrity questioned, and his abilities sneered at, by those who had recently extolled them. In short, Mr. Van Buren encountered, in the earliest period of his career, an earnest of that malignant and persevering abuse with which he has been incessantly assailed, from that time to the present." At a time when the worst that could be said of someone was that he admired the French Revolution, Van Buren was likened to Marat and Robespierre. Hard as it must have been, he never turned back. From that moment forward, Van Buren would be a democrat, and a well-dressed one to boot.

Fortunately, there was another influential family in Kinderhook, and they leaned Jeffersonian. The Van Ness clan included two young brothers, John and William, who took an interest in the young clerk. Van Buren showed early signs of his political abilities by helping John win nomination to Congress at a caucus in nearby Troy, and as his reward he was sent to New York City to live and study with William, an up-and-coming Republican lawyer. He arrived there in 1801, his own destiny tied to the new century and to the Empire City about to explode into existence.

It would have been hard to dream up a better situation for Van Buren. Though young, William Van Ness was an intimate of the great luminary of New York politics, Vice President Aaron Burr, the cynosure of all eyes in those years before the duel at Weehawken. Burr was only forty-five years old in 1801, but he had lived enough for most men. A grandson of Jonathan Edwards; hero of the Revolution; founder of Tammany Hall; and very nearly president after the disputed election of 1800, he was now using his formidable powers of persuasion to line up supporters among the talented young men swarming to New York. Van Ness was one of the chief lieutenants of Burr's "Little Band"—he would serve as Burr's second during the fateful duel with Hamilton—and consequently Van Buren was often in the presence of the great man.

These must have been thrilling days for Van Buren—not yet twenty years old, living in Manhattan, savoring the moment when political supremacy tilted away from the Federalists, and through it all, enjoying the attention of the brilliant vice president of the United States, a man he resembled enough to cause tongues to wag. If they were not related, then they certainly enjoyed an ideological kinship. Even fifty years later, Van Buren seemed to relish every glance as he recalled Burr in his memoir: "He treated me with much attention, and my sympathies were excited by his subsequent position."*

The rumor is worth discussing, not only because rumors can be as significant as facts, but because there is a passing resemblance between the young Van Buren and the rake whispered to be his true father. But is it true? Most scholars have scoffed at the story, but for an implausible reason: because Van Buren's mother, thirty-five when he was born, with a few kids already, and stuck in a tavern, was presumably unattractive to Burr. Such an assumption assumes that (a) middle-aged women exercise no sex appeal and (b) Aaron Burr only liked women of great beauty. The first assumption is subjective and dangerous, and there is no merit to the second, either.

But having established Burr's right to enjoy carnal relations with anyone he chose, there are still problems with the theory that he fathered Van Buren. No one seems to have mentioned it until it was harmful to Van Buren's career. And when push came to shove, Van Buren was not much of an ally to Burr, once again bucking a mentor. In November 1803, Van Buren passed the bar and moved back to Kinderhook to hang out his shingle with his half brother. A few months later, Burr ran for governor of New York as an independent candidate. Despite his admiration for Burr, Van Buren cast his vote with the regular nominee of the Republicans, Morgan Lewis. The Van Ness family was apoplectic, and when Van Buren arrived to vote, they publicly challenged his right to vote, an "indignity" he did not forget but which he overlooked several months later when William Van Ness needed legal help to avoid being arrested after the Hamilton-Burr duel. A poignant scene in his memoir describes Van Buren knocking as hard as he can on the door of the Van Ness

---

*Surprisingly, he also described with rapt attention his chance presence at a "great speech" given by Hamilton against Burr, thrilling with the recollection that "my seat was so near to Hamilton that I could hear distinctly every word he said."

mansion, and the senior Van Ness refusing to answer the door, but smiling at Van Buren's audacity. Half a century later, still audacious, Van Buren would buy the Van Ness house outright for himself.

Van Buren was learning that friends could be as difficult as enemies and that politics was a blood sport. He was also gaining a grasp of how the battle was practiced up close. An interesting letter he wrote in 1802 describes a hard-fought election in which the Republicans were nearly outfoxed by the Federalists, whose "wagons were continually going fetching the Lame the blind & the aged to the poll." Van Buren's side, needless to add, was "not wanting in activity," and "not even the Machiavellian arts of Federalism [could] withstand the Irresistible ardor of Freedom of Republicans." In other words, Van Buren's side won—probably by fighting even dirtier than their opponents.

Van Buren's political activity grew alongside his legal career in Kinderhook. Throughout the long presidency of Thomas Jefferson, Van Buren reveled in the spread of democratic principles. Describing this period, a sentence in his memoir hints at how deep-seated his convictions were: "My faith in the capacity of the masses of the People of our Country to govern themselves, and in their general integrity in the exercise of that function, was very decided and was more and more strengthened as my intercourse with them extended." A contemporary recorded Van Buren's enthusiasm for Jefferson: "His support of the government was not merely active but zealous; nor was his the zeal of ordinary men. It absorbed his whole soul; it led to untiring exertion; it was exhibited on all occasions and under all circumstances. Neither the contumely of inflated wealth, not the opposition of invidious talent, nor the revilings of a licentious press, could awe it into silence or soften it to moderation."

In 1807, there were a number of challenges to his worldview. Another bruising election brought out the fissures in the unstable foundation of New York politics. That year, Van Buren supported the regular nominee of his party for governor, the popular Daniel

Tompkins—known far and wide as "the Farmer's Boy." But once again most of Kinderhook lined up behind personal factions, and there was anger on all sides. A more disciplined party organization was desperately needed.

Van Buren was not yet able to offer that discipline, but he took a dramatic step toward the organization of his personal life in that year. On February 21, 1807, he married Hannah Hoes in Catskill, New York. In the Van Buren family tradition, she was a first cousin once removed (her grandfather was Van Buren's uncle) and native to Kinderhook. Soon, he would have a growing family along with a growing practice—nine months later, the first of his four sons was born. In the long annals of the presidency, it would be difficult to find a presidential spouse we know less about than Hannah Van Buren. There are no likenesses of her, and she died long before Van Buren was elected. She is not mentioned in the enormous manuscript of his autobiography. Yet there is not the slightest whiff of scandal about their love, and it is telling that he never remarried after her death in 1819.

It was an auspicious time to start a new life with his bride. Later that same year, Robert Fulton's steamboat *Clermont* traveled from New York City to Albany in thirty-two hours. The Hudson Valley would never be the same. To get even closer to the water highway and the business it brought, Van Buren moved his practice to the new town of Hudson, just south of Kinderhook. Soon he was making $10,000 a year, and creating a stir as one of the most gifted lawyers in a remarkable constellation of Hudson River attorneys.

We have lost the sense of what the law once stood for to ambitious young men. As the nineteenth century dawned, it still commanded an awe that transcended the political realm. Lawyers were the priests of a secular order. Their learning was majestic: their Latinate vocabularies, their parchments, their stately mien, their effortless command of the Common Law, the repository of Anglo-Saxon cultural habits dating back half a millennium. The United States may have been writing a new chapter in human history, but its lawyers, the people who really ran things, were part of an ancient guild connecting them to the Middle Ages. Tocqueville wrote, with understatement, "The government of democracy is favorable to the political power of lawyers."

In a brief posthumous memoir of Van Buren, his family friend William Allen Butler conveyed the nineteenth-century sense that an attorney is somehow apart from mortal men, endowed with luminous, unearthly powers like those we now reserve for comic-book superheroes:

> A true lawyer is always a lawyer. If he gives himself wholly to the severe discipline which is the condition of success, and gains the secrets of that science which, more than all other human forces, directs the progress of events, its subtle light surrounds him like an atmosphere, and accompanies him like a perpetual presence.

It does not appear that Van Buren ever considered another career, and well into his political career he was practicing law on the side. Even before he left school, Van Buren conducted mock trials with friends. There is a story, perhaps apocryphal, that relates a dazzling early legal performance when he was only a teenager, practicing at law against a much older sparring partner, and had to be helped up to stand on a table in his address to the jury. Either he was impressively young, or just very short. Now, in adulthood, all his talents came to the fore. His nose for research, his memory, and his shrewd common sense endowed him with a formidable ability in the courtroom.

Van Buren was fortunate to have a Hudson Valley rival every bit as formidable in Elisha Williams, a staunch Federalist and, more often than not, the agent of the great families against whom Van Buren was invariably opposed. A newspaper once attacked Williams for his snobbery, complaining that he "disliked the ring-streaked and speckled population of our large towns and cities, comprising people of every kind and tongue." Williams reserved some of that contempt for his ambitious adversary. He wrote waspishly, "Poor little Matty. What a blessing it is for one to think he is the greatest little fellow in the world. It would be cruel to compel this man to estimate himself correctly." The "little fellow" would soon cut Williams down to size.

As this remark suggests, Williams was tall and grand, Van Buren compact and merely diligent. Benjamin Butler, Van Buren's old friend, enjoyed the comparison:

> Never were two men more dissimilar. Both were eloquent; but the eloquence of Williams was declamatory and exciting, that of Van Buren insinuating and delightful. Williams had the livelier imagination, Van Buren the sounder judgment. The former presented the strong points of his case in bolder relief, invested them with a more brilliant coloring, indulged a more unlicensed and magnificent invective, and gave more life and variety to his arguments by his peculiar wit and inimitable humor; but Van Buren was his superior in analyzing, arranging and combining the insulated materials, in comparing and weighing testimony, in unraveling the web of intricate affairs, in eviscerating truth from the mass of diversified and conflicting evidence, in softening the heart and molding it to his purpose and in working into the judgments of his hearers the conclusions of his own perspicuous and persuasive reasonings.

Over time, Van Buren prevailed more often than not, and as he did so, he began to develop the resources that would allow him to conquer so many others who would underestimate him. In retrospect, the skills Van Buren honed in the courtroom were identical to those he would apply to the political world. Preparation, hard work, and plain language—those were the earthy ingredients in the

Little Magician's alchemical brew. A lucky break came when he was able to buy the law library of an attorney and rectify some of his educational flaws by reading voraciously at night. Slowly, he made a name for himself as a debater to be reckoned with, and soon, inevitably, he was using his legal talents to torture his social superiors.

Like all lawyers, Van Buren took the different cases that came his way. To some extent, he had no choice, for he admitted, "I was not worth a shilling when I commenced my professional career." But a clear pattern was discernible. Generally, he defended the lower and middling orders that he had sprung from, and went on the attack against a social order that was nowhere near as democratic as the American Revolution would suggest. Specifically, he made his business the investigation of the huge patroon land grants, revealing his conviction that there were improprieties in the old claims that benefited the wealthy families and defrauded the small freeholders. The stakes were high and emotions ran high as well—Van Buren was even challenged to a duel by an agent for the Van Rensselaers (the duel never took place). Through his effective work, Van Buren drew "an opposition at once powerful, personal and peculiar."

All of Van Buren's early biographers, the ones who knew him, agreed on the centrality of this experience. George Bancroft wrote, with perfervid prose, that "the farmer's son from Kinderhook" had led the fight against "the claimants under ancient warrants." William Allen Butler went one better by writing, "It was the old story of Richard and Saladin." In his account, Van Buren almost single-handedly defeated "the Federalists of Columbia County, who had money, lands, and a kind of patrician pride; who believed in their own capacity to govern everybody, and disbelieved in the capacity of other people to govern themselves."

Obviously, some of these memories were a little skewed, and there was no reason to drag Saladin in. Van Buren was not Richard the Lionheart and never would be. But he was well suited to the battle he had found. He liked to win, and he was good at it, which often enraged his opponents, especially since he was taking away power that they felt was their birthright. He won with his eloquence, his facts, and his street smarts. All three would come in handy as he climbed the political ladder. All would enrage his opponents, unaccustomed to losing, and would lay the groundwork for the attacks on Van Buren that never ceased throughout his incredibly long public career. As he put it, bluntly, "I was an eye-sore to the Magnates."

Each apprenticeship seemed to prepare him for the next stage. He was learning prodigiously, and meeting more and more luminaries from outside Columbia County. Just as Lincoln would do in Illinois, he traveled the circuit, talking about people and politics everywhere he went. One source claims that he was developing a useful skill for a politician—the ability to walk into a tavern and hold an enormous amount of alcohol without any sign of impairment.

Obviously, it was only a matter of time before this young attorney committed to his true calling. If Van Buren was mild-mannered, he was still intensely ambitious, a fact that none of his supporters ever denied and which his enemies were quick to point out as a flaw. In 1812, Van Buren ran for the state senate, and profited from his new reputation as a champion of the people to win the Republican nomination from two wealthier candidates. His election opponent was Edward Livingston, the scion of another great New York family and the apparent favorite for the seat.

Although Van Buren could command the votes of the main body of Republican voters, the early results suggested that Livingston had won. Van Buren climbed aboard a steamboat at Hudson and prepared to resume his legal career by attending the spring session at New York City. "Whilst I was arranging my luggage and my papers, my opponents, headed by the leading men of my county, were celebrating their supposed victory at the Hotel on the opposite side of the street, and when I left my door the most jubilant among them appeared on the piazza and shed upon me, at parting, the light of their beaming countenances."

Then, as the boat passed Catskill, Van Buren noticed his brother-in-law waving from shore and pointing to a small rowboat making its way toward the steamer. It was bringing the news that Van Buren had won more votes than at first counted, and had eked out victory by fewer than 200 votes out of 40,000 cast. It was appropriate that he received the news on a steamboat, symbolic of the contrivances that were taking men of the nineteenth century to places they had never been before. He called this moment "my political birth and baptism." At twenty-nine, he was the second youngest senator ever elected in New York. From then until the end of his presidency, he would serve almost continuously in government service.

This, then, was a worthy beginning. Kinderhook would mark Van Buren forever. It had given him a wife, a family, countless friends, a career, and more than a few enemies. It had brought him into contact with the humble, the great, and the mass of people in between. It had taught him how much America offers to a youth of talent and how much it can take out of someone who seeks more power than he is offered. It had taught him to speak for himself, and to speak for others like him, to be willing to stand up for principles against those who were all for democracy as long as it was restricted to themselves. All in all, it was a good place to begin.

2

Regency

In 1842, Jabez Hammond published *The History of Political Parties in the State of New York*, in three octavo volumes. If you can even find it in a library, there is a good chance that you will be the first person to have taken it out in a century and a half. Yet beneath its ancient leather binding, the brittle pages teem with life. Hammond's saga explores the sinuous windings of New York politics across three generations, at the dawn of the republican experiment. Aaron Spelling could hardly ask for more: colossal egos in conflict, visionary acts of statecraft, and the petty acts of villainy that no less truly define our politics. In short, Hammond tells the story of democracy's journey from idea to thing. For the patient reader, its hieroglyphics offer a Rosetta stone, translating the long-lost world of the early republic into something comprehensible and restoring our sense that the founders, for all their idealism, were also men of the world, given to selfishness like any other generation. Despite his dated language, Hammond ranks with A. J. Liebling, Edwin O'Connor, and Robert Penn Warren as a chronicler of the American political process. His secret hero is Martin Van Buren, who ushered in the new world and gave a kick in the pants to the old.

Van Buren's term in the New York Senate began on the Fourth

of July, 1812. He made the most of the opportunity, and then some. He arrived at the Senate "dressed in a green coat, buff breeches, and white topped boots, and withal bearing himself somewhat jauntily." He never looked back. Within a decade he would become the undisputed master of New York at the precise moment that New York was beginning the unchecked growth that would place the Empire State at the center of American politics for a century and more.

That was not the only respect in which the young senator's timing was excellent. Almost exactly as he took office, the War of 1812 erupted, the unfortunate collision of insulting English behavior toward Americans on the high seas and war fever among jingoistic young politicians who were just beginning to make a name for themselves—John Calhoun of South Carolina, Henry Clay of Kentucky, and many others from the South and West, where war was remote and therefore romantic.

For New Yorkers, war with Great Britain was anything but a daydream. The conflict could not have been more immediate, not only for its disruption of commerce, but also for the fact that New York was a principal theater throughout the hostilities. Just as they had twenty-five years earlier, British troops menaced New Yorkers from all directions. They burned Buffalo, they attacked shipping on the Great Lakes, they threatened Lake Champlain and the upper Hudson, and for three long years they committed strikes along the entire length of the endless Canadian border. To make matters worse, New England was on the verge of secession, and the national leadership in Washington was divided and weak. New York was caught in the middle of a bad situation.

But if the war was severely disruptive, it also presented an unusual opportunity for a young organizational wizard. Like so many he would later spar with (Jackson, Calhoun, Clay, Harrison, Cass), Van Buren came out of the war with a larger reputation. For the rest of his life, he would measure friends and rivals by their bellicosity in 1812. Even before his election, he had spoken out against England, and his ardor for the war effort was increased by the fact that this was another way to stick it to the Federalists, whose support for Republican foreign policy was lukewarm at best.

After the war broke out, Van Buren quickly threw himself into the defense of New York, America, and democracy—and an address he gave in 1813 shows that he considered all three to be one and the same. This was no mere struggle for military advantage—he felt that the very idea of republicanism was under assault from the hated British. (And we should not forget that for the Dutch-speaking Van Buren, the British were always foreigners.) "The only free people on earth," living in "the last republic," needed to stand up now and prove "whether man is capable of self-government, whether our republic must go the way of its predecessors." "The eyes of the world are directed towards us," with democracy hinging on the result. Opposing these manly thoughts were "the seductive wiles and blandishments of the corrupt minions of aristocracy"—a phrase that might apply to the patroons as well as to the British.

After a critical election swung support to the Republicans, an emergency session of the legislature was called in September 1814 to shore up support for what appeared to be a losing war effort. Only two weeks before the session, an American naval victory on Lake Champlain had thwarted a British advance, or otherwise the British might have been passing laws in Albany. The result of this scare was a flurry of desperate war measures to raise troops and money, the centerpiece of which was Van Buren's Classification Bill, a bold proposal to allow New York to conscript twelve thousand white men between the ages of eighteen and forty-five. Intriguingly, the young legislator had help from an old friend—Aaron Burr, who helped him to draft the fairly radical legislation. The bill passed through the frightened assembly, and would have been put into effect if not mooted by the end of the war in early 1815. Thomas Hart Benton called it "the most energetic war measure ever adopted in our America." Political enemies would do their best later on to make fun of the fact that Van Buren had not distinguished himself on the field of battle, but he had made a genuine contribution, and Benton wrote that news of the Classification Bill was received in Washington "with an exultation only inferior to that with which was received the news of the victory of New Orleans." Another wise move was a public resolution Van Buren offered in the happy aftermath of the Battle of New Orleans, praising "Major General Jackson, his gallant officers and troops, for their wonderful, and heroic victory in defence of the grand emporium of the West." That, too, would come in handy.

For these and other reasons that we may never fully understand, power began to flow to Van Buren, remarkably swiftly. It was not merely that he was prescient in supporting people who would help him later. He was also a gifted legislator, comfortable in the salons where deals were struck, quick to see how one favor might lead to another. He was unfailingly easy to get along with, as even his enemies admitted. He was a workhorse, rising at 4:30 in the morning. He could count votes faster than any of his peers, and quietly arrange for members to arrive or disappear at the last moment to tilt a vote one way or the other.

He also chose good issues to identify himself with. From the moment he started his career, he was the friend of the small farmer. As Franklin Roosevelt would do a century later, he tried to ease the credit burden on rural producers who were cash poor. In particular, he lashed out at the common practice of imprisonment for debt, which in his opinion was the same thing as a jail sentence "for the misfortune of being poor, of being unable to satisfy the all-digesting stomach of some ravenous creditor." It was this campaign, rather extraordinarily, that would provoke Ezra Pound to poetic rapture at a time when Van Buren's name was all but forgotten. His thirty-seventh canto begins, "'Thou shalt not,' said Martin Van Buren, 'jail 'em for debt.'" Van Buren also vehemently opposed the rechartering of the Bank of the United States in 1812, not only because it concentrated resources in a relatively small number of hands, but because so many of its supporters were Federalists. And he continued to snipe at the great landed families.

As Van Buren quickly climbed the ladder, it became clear to him that the chaotic state of New York politics was in itself a reason that legislative progress had been slow on the issues that mattered to his constituents. He sensed that the state was ready for a new politics, more tightly organized, quicker to pounce. As he discovered the issues that mattered to him, and the politicians who shared his sentiments, he naturally begin to think of harnessing them together as a new organization. It could not have escaped his attention that the large numbers of people coming into New York would provide even further support once their votes could be counted.

Of course, there had been earlier political organizations in New York, led by the great figures of the founding generation. It would be hard to think of more charismatic leaders than Hamilton, who invented the Federalist Party, or Burr, who founded Tammany Hall. Van Buren could not match them for personality. But in effect, that was precisely the point—personality was irrelevant to a smooth-functioning machine, and that is what he set out to build. The Careful Dutchman had an instinctive sense of how to create an organization. If he had grown up in Lowell, Massachusetts, he would have become a textile tycoon. In New York, faster than any other politician of his day, he learned how to harness a far greater source of power than the mill races of the Merrimack River—the people themselves.

It has never been easy to offer a simple tour through the thickets and brambles of New York politics, then or now. John Calhoun once sighed that the state's politics "have always been a great deep." Van Buren's great contribution was to impose a new order on them, and the party that he began to fashion in the 1810s and 1820s is more accurately the ancestor of the modern Democratic Party than Thomas Jefferson's Republicans, though Jefferson gets all of the credit.

He was simply the right man for the right moment. The Federalists, founded with a burst of energy in the 1790s, were increasingly out of touch with the rapidly changing American scene. It was not simply that they had handled themselves poorly during the war, it was the disappearance of an entire culture that had nurtured them. Life had accelerated appreciably in the first two decades of the nineteenth century. Steamboats plied the waters of New York harbor; new mercantile concerns sent ships around the world; investments in the West brought untold riches to those who made them wisely. The center of this new capital and new energy was of course Manhattan, but its effects could be felt in the farthest reaches of the Empire State. As such, the old politics of personal influence, dominated by great families, was coming to an end. There would be no more uncles arranging favors for nephews with nosebleeds.

Van Buren set about building a disciplined political organization, driven by strict loyalty, careful working out of positions, and reasonable meritocracy. His efficiency sounded the death knell of the ancien régime, and they loathed him for it. In 1824 the last patroon, Stephen Van Rensselaer, complained bitterly, "Party mixes with every question." Four years later, he retired from politics because party battles "are too disgusting for my Ear as I have ever kept good company. Vulgarity disgusts me." Even when former Federalists tried to enlist with Van Buren, they didn't quite fit in.

But as Van Buren made his way in the world, he also noticed that the path to glory was crowded. One obstacle, in particular, loomed larger than all the others. In the second decade of the nineteenth century, voters were blinded by the bright sun of a personality who dominated New York politics—De Witt Clinton, the "Magnus Apollo." Clinton, the nephew of former governor George Clinton, was mayor of New York and a former senator. For over a decade he had dazzled voters and politicians alike with his confidence and vision—although he had put off more than a few of them with his arrogance. He was a difficult politician to categorize—wealthy in his background and taste, he voted Jeffersonian on most issues and did not suffer fools gladly. Clinton knew his worth and felt not only that New York should take the presidency away from Virginia, but that he should be the person to do it.

At first, Van Buren and Clinton were friendly. Clinton helped with his election, and as soon as Van Buren entered the state senate, he supported Clinton's drive to unseat James Madison and run for the White House in 1812. It was a difficult cause for Van Buren to champion, for it involved a temporary alliance with New York Federalists, and Van Buren had to resort to some electoral trickery to swing New York's delegation behind Clinton—exactly the sort of maneuver that would later arouse suspicion.

Predictably, the quixotic bid failed, and as Clinton resumed his imperious ways, Van Buren grew annoyed with him. To some extent, the rupture emanated from Van Buren's sense that Clinton was lying to him. But surely there were other reasons, and none may have been simpler than the fact that each saw in the other a dangerous rival. A biographer who was close to Van Buren, William Allen Butler, once said that he was "guided by an intellect which looked into the centre of things, and into the secrets of men." Somehow, when he looked at Clinton, he saw something that he didn't like. A small clue may come from the dismissive tone that Clinton used to derogate a letter that Van Buren had written, calling it "equally offensive to grammar and to truth." That was the language a wealthy gentleman used to humiliate his manservant, and it must have cut Van Buren deeply. A nineteenth-century biographer wrote that their struggle had "something of the gall and wormwood of a family quarrel."

In a way, they were the opposite of each other. Clinton, well born, oversized, still had some of the characteristics of the eighteenth century—the century of great families, great deeds, and individual glory. Van Buren, diminutive, with superior organizational skills, was already planning the nineteenth century. Clinton was a popular leader, but erratic, often forming temporary alliances that diluted his politics. Van Buren saw the party as inviolate, and was disturbed by the caprices of Clinton's leadership. Their personalities were different as well. An observer wrote, "Mr. Clinton was reserved in manner, but gave free utterance to his thoughts,—Mr. Van Buren was frank in manner, but concealed his thoughts. Mr. Clinton was always bold and decided,—Mr. Van Buren only so at the proper time. The former studied books,—the latter men. The one could scarcely control himself, much less govern others; the other was complete master of himself, and therefore, easily obtained the mastery over others."

Inevitably, they began to oppose each other, although in such a stealthy way that it was rarely clear who had the upper hand or who, in fact, was trying to do what to the other. With his usual efficiency, Van Buren set out to diminish Clinton's influence, to enlarge his own, and to build a durable party structure that would brush aside individual idiosyncrasies in favor of larger goals. The break came in 1813, when Clinton asked Van Buren to renominate him for lieutenant governor, and Van Buren gave such a sarcastic speech about Clinton that it was clear he was his enemy. Clinton called him "that prince of villains." He was the first in a long line of strong political personalities who would butt heads with Van Buren and walk away wondering how he had lost.

Strengthened by the war effort, Van Buren was elected attorney general in 1815 and began to gather around him a host of talented young supporters, following the model Aaron Burr had set fifteen years earlier. They were loosely bound by their dislike for Clinton, but they also seem to have genuinely liked each other. These young lawyers and journalists, often both at the same time, increasingly looked to Van Buren as their leader. They included men who would form the core of the New York Democracy: Benjamin Butler, John Edmonds, William L. Marcy, and the future senator and governor Silas Wright. Some came to Van Buren simply as law clerks; others he found during his frequent trips around the state. According to Silas Wright's amusing account, he met Van Buren after he accidentally pushed him into the water during a ferry ride. They would become lifelong friends.

Between 1817 and 1821, these sympathetic friends cohered into a more sophisticated political organization than New York had ever known. They developed a clear party ideology, they were loyal to one another, and they used the press brilliantly to explain themselves. Back in 1813, in his first year as a state senator, Van Buren had helped to found a newspaper, the *Albany Argus*, and in 1820 he became one of the paper's chief investors. At first, Clinton's opponents were loosely characterized as "the Bucktails," after a hat worn by Tammany Hall supporters. As Van Buren's new party gained more power, they also attracted more sophisticated names. Some called them "the Holy Alliance," but the name that eventually stuck, coined by the young journalist Thurlow Weed, was "the Albany Regency." Weed wrote, "I do not believe that a stronger political combination ever existed at any state capital, or even at the national capital. They were men of great ability, great industry, indomitable courage, and strict personal integrity."

Simply put, the party wanted to return to Jeffersonian principles, but to do so in a way that was consonant with New York's extraordinary growth. They wanted to defend small farmers from predatory special interests, but they also drew strength from the mounting population of New York City. They were philosophically opposed to large government expenditures but, after some soul-searching, came to support the biggest public project of the era—the Erie Canal, also known as "Clinton's Ditch" in honor of De Witt Clinton. After Van Buren overcame his early objections, he gave an emotionally charged speech defending the project. For all their difficulties, Clinton and Van Buren shook hands.

It is odd that we now call this the Era of Good Feelings. So many disgruntled politicians were working to destroy one another, and the absence of a two-party system did little to foster civility. Jabez Hammond wrote that "the party spirit had raged more in this than in any other state in the union," and he blamed it on the great temptation to give jobs to friends, a practice Clinton excelled in, but which Van Buren also enjoyed. Despite their truce over the Erie Canal, Clinton and Van Buren continued to build rival factions, both nominally Republican but clearly different. They struggled for dominance for a decade. When Clinton was riding high, he laughed at Van Buren's misfortune, comparing him to an old Flemish painting of Jonah, expectorated by the whale, and "having a very bewildered and dismal physiognomy, not knowing from whence he came nor to what place bound." On another occasion, he described him as a torpid serpent, lulled to sleep by a favor, "but if you warm him he will sting." Van Buren returned the compliment, calling Clinton "the snake." Clinton's ascent to the governor's mansion in 1817 was a severe setback for Van Buren, and he entered political purgatory for a time.

One year was especially difficult. On February 5, 1819, Hannah Van Buren died of tuberculosis, leaving the thirty-six-year-old Van Buren a widower with four sons. His father and mother had died not long before. Van Buren stayed home for a week after the funeral, physically and emotionally depleted. Later that year, he was removed from his position as attorney general. He was nearly appointed to the state Supreme Court, but before he could consider the proposal, it was vetoed by the governor—De Witt Clinton. Van Buren had reached a low ebb. Hammond believed that if Van Buren had been tendered this position, he would have voluntarily removed himself from elective politics forever. "He appeared to be tired of the eternal political struggles to which he seemed doomed, and such, in truth, he told me was the fact," Hammond wrote.

It was a difficult year for another reason. The proposed admission of Missouri to the Union excited an unprecedented noise over what would become the great dilemma of American history. In February 1819, a New York congressman, James Tallmadge, proposed an amendment barring the further introduction of slaves into

Missouri. A series of speeches by New York senator Rufus King followed, excoriating the spread of slavery as dangerous to the Union. King was an especially powerful advocate, having attended the Constitutional Convention in 1787, and, as John Quincy Adams recorded, "the great slaveholders in the House gnawed their lips and clutched their fists as they heard him."

As usual, New York was right in the middle of this national debate. Although King was an old Federalist, he and Van Buren were friendly, drawn together by their mutual distrust of De Witt Clinton. Van Buren went along with the growing anti-slavery movement in New York, too far for some and not far enough for many. He signed his name to a list of people calling for a meeting on Missouri in Albany, but he did not attend the actual meeting and used his failure to attend as a pretext for not signing the anti-slavery document produced by the meeting. When he ran for president in 1836, fact-checkers would pore over these early events in New York to look for signs that Van Buren had acted decisively for or against the peculiar institution: they all came away empty-handed.

Partly because of Van Buren's growing friendship with anti-Clinton Federalists like King, and partly because of the rising sophistication of his methods, the Bucktails were poised to make great gains in 1820, a year after his nadir. They had held their first caucus as a separate party in 1819 and ran well against the Clintonians, aided by the press organs they had founded. In 1821, Van Buren ran for the U.S. Senate and won a difficult victory. That same year, his allies swept into the state council of appointment, which controlled the patronage of New York, and cherry-picked jobs for their supporters. The tide was turning.

But there was one last piece of unfinished business that Van Buren needed to make his mastery of New York complete. The state constitution, written in 1777, was woefully inadequate for the changing times, and a number of its archaic features favored Clinton's autocratic style of government—particularly the power of appointment. The Bucktails proposed a constitutional convention to rewrite it, and the public voted its approval. Beginning on August 28, 1821, the convention dramatically rewrote the rules of New York government, enlarged the suffrage from 100,000 to 260,000, reduced the governor's tenure from three to two years, reformed the patronage and judiciary systems, and generally accepted the idea that parties can govern more efficiently than individuals. These were heady changes, but as Van Buren said, "That which ought to be done ought to be done quickly."

Van Buren was not the author of all of these changes, nor did he go along with all of them. He was generally moderate, steering between extremes of conservatism ["some dozen hare-brained politicians"] and radicalism ["a small number of Mad-caps"] as the new order was forming. One of his more famous sayings dated from this time—that government should not be guided by "temporary excitement" but by the "sober second thought" of the people. But there was no doubt about who was in command, and who was the principal beneficiary of the new system that was forming. The changes were not perfect—and notably, they did not do much to extend the vote to black freemen (Van Buren fought those who would deny blacks the vote, but he went along with a requirement that they own $250, which removed many of them from the rolls). But the new constitution loosened up a sclerotic system so that it could cope with the rapid pace of the times, and in a sense it gave the vote not only to the people who suddenly received it in the 1820s, but to all those who would receive it every time the suffrage was enlarged. The New York Constitutional Convention established a vital principle around the nation: the democracy created on the Fourth of July was fluid, not static. The Revolution continued.

As he prepared to go to Washington, Van Buren could look back on a decade of extraordinary political growth. From his election as state senator in 1812, he had quickly established himself in Albany, tangled with the Magnus Apollo and won more often than he lost. He had helped save New York's honor during the dark days of the War of 1812. He had met the supporters who would follow him up and down the mountain over the next two decades. And he had forever changed the way the people of his state governed themselves.

Even more profoundly, Van Buren had laid the foundation for what would become Jacksonian Democracy in only a few short years. With his ideas about party discipline, communications, and enlarged suffrage, he had shown other like-minded individuals how to take democracy beyond the periwigs of the eighteenth century. His ascent in New York coincided perfectly with New York's emergence as the most important state in the Union. Everyone knew that New York City was growing rapidly. Whoever controlled New York's electoral votes would have more and more to say about who became president. The Kinderhooker had become a kingmaker.

Van Buren's rival De Witt Clinton had done well over the same ten years, and deservedly received accolades for the Erie Canal, nearing completion in 1821 (finished in 1825). But in truth, it was the Dutchman whose future stretched far over the horizon. Now, in 1821, Van Buren's work in New York was done. The Regency would govern his native state for him while he was away. It was time to turn to the rest of the country.

3

Democracy

As the newly elected senator Van Buren wended his way toward Washington, there were precious few reasons to expect that he would enjoy the same success that he had found in New York politics. At home, a Byzantine in Byzantium, he had deciphered the local bureaucracy and prevailed against formidable enemies. But the national stage was vast, unfamiliar, and unforgiving. Those who dominated it possessed qualities that were foreign to him—stentorian voices, aristocratic noses, generous estates. His talents, at first glance, would seem more congenial to the House of Representatives than to the Roman Senate. But once again he would trump the cynics. Within seven years, he created the modern Democratic Party, anointed Andrew Jackson as its standard-bearer, and revolutionized American politics forever.

Van Buren arrived in Washington on November 5, 1821. Within a few hours of his arrival, as if the political weather had already changed, he received his first visit, from an operator every bit as skillful as he—John C. Calhoun of South Carolina, the secretary of war. Their meeting was friendly, and soon Van Buren was playing whist with the great Southron and his friends. Calhoun, already casting an eye on the White House, was transparently hoping to use Van Buren to advance his presidential hopes. But for all their pretended friendliness, something intangible separated them—party doctrine, perhaps, or simply the fact that each was there blocking the other. Despite periodic alliances, they would never trust each other, and in that distrust were planted the seeds of the great sectional tensions that would engulf the Union four decades later. Failing to become great friends, they instead became mortal enemies.

Washington was hardly the seat of an empire in 1821. Nothing proclaimed that fact quite as vividly as the scorch marks on the White House from its immolation in 1814. Farther down Pennsylvania Avenue, the Capitol lurched upward, ungainly and unfinished, its incompletion an apt metaphor for the nation it symbolized. Washington was no Rome—it contained a grand total of 23,000 people, and a disconcerting number of them (7,000) were enslaved. A traveling Englishman called it "the most forlorn and melancholy place, bearing the value of a capital, I ever was in."

But tawdriness was never a problem for the now-elegant Van Buren, who moved easily in his new surroundings and made friends quickly. His reputation as an arch-politician preceded him, and his messmate Rufus King predicted that "within two weeks Van Buren will become perfectly acquainted with the views and feelings of every member, yet no man will know his." Unfortunately, there was a setback with his maiden speech in the Senate. Ambitiously, he chose a topic that had nothing to do with New York—a Louisiana land transaction—as if to show that he was no mere hick from upstate New York, and the fact that it dealt with issues of false titles must have brought him back to his early days arguing on behalf of the small farmers of Kinderhook. But with all of Washington watching, disaster struck. Van Buren launched his campaign for political supremacy by giving what may have been the worst debut performance in the history of the Senate. He suffered a "break down," in his own words, lost his way in the speech, and sat down confused and humiliated—a feeling that any high-school elocution-ist will instantly recognize. In his memoir, not exactly the most readable political document ever written, he was unusually moving when describing this moment, confessing that for all his success, he had never been free from great "timidity" and "embarrassment" in his public speaking. But it seemed to matter very little. As his adversary taunted him, Van Buren rediscovered his voice in a fit of anger, and ultimately won the debate. Before long, he was comfortable in the Senate, and especially with the Old Republicans who still felt loyal to the ancient ideals of Thomas Jefferson, somewhat dimly remembered as the third decade of the nineteenth century opened. Soon Van Buren was chairman of the Judiciary Committee, and well on his way to reinventing the political system.

Those who knew him well could verify that this had been his secret ambition from the start. An unpublished diary by a New York acquaintance, Charlemagne Tower, records Van Buren as saying privately that he planned to "revive the old contest between the federals and the anti-federals and build up a party for himself." In his correspondence, he admitted that his great goal was the "resuscitation of the old democratic party," using the same techniques he had learned in Albany on the national stage. It was a shockingly audacious plan, especially coming from a first-year senator. And while it was couched in careful Jeffersonian language, what Van Buren had in mind was nothing less than the organization of a new party, unprecedented in power and reach.

Progress was slow at first. Van Buren got into some early patronage squabbles with the Monroe administration, which exacerbated the distrust he already felt toward the president. His tidy Dutch mind hated the disorderliness of the national political scene in the early 1820s. Great changes were in the air, and it was becoming obvious that George Washington's fantasy of a single party was inadequate for the governance of what was no longer a simple rural republic. The argument over the admission of Missouri had revealed just how deep feelings ran over slavery, both North and South. Economic and diplomatic policies changed as you traveled over the map. Dozens of personality cults had grown in Washington—little cabals dedicated to electing their leaders to higher office and willing to stop at nothing to do it.

Van Buren yearned to impose some order on this mess. In particular, he distrusted Monroe, who claimed to be a Republican, but had too many former Federalists around him for Van Buren's taste. New York's new senator felt strongly that the party was being weakened, not strengthened, by this "fusion policy," and that everything it once stood for was being watered down by aimless "amalgamation." This was political déjà vu—for Van Buren had run the same campaign against De Witt Clinton in New York, when he transformed the upstart Bucktails into the Regency by drilling into them the great value of party regularity. Once again, he set to work, building alliances, emphasizing the need for a disciplined platform, and using his base in New York to command respect from all parts of the Union—especially from the large flock of presidential aspirants craving New York's electoral votes.

Will Rogers once said, "I don't belong to an organized party— I'm a Democrat." But, in fact, organization is precisely what distinguished the proto-party that Van Buren was forming. Far beyond anything that had existed before, Van Buren envisioned a national structure, tethered together by speedy communications and tight message control, that would unite the aspirations of "the planters of the South and the plain Republicans of the North." It was the Regency reanimated—only on a far bigger scale. From across the Union, the people would be connected by alert local committees reporting to their state chairmen, but, just as importantly, by the novel sense that politics was a participatory ritual, gaudy and fun. It took a tavernkeeper's son to figure out that the American people actually like being with each other.

We have grown so complacent with the idea of two-party democracy that we still fail to grasp its revolutionary power. There is nothing in the Constitution about opposition parties and, in fact, the Founding Fathers took great pains to express their horror for them. James Madison attacked "the violence of faction" in Federalist 10 (though he was not above joining the first party squabbles of the 1790s), and George Washington, even more shrilly, denounced "the baneful effects of the Spirit of Party" in his farewell address. Considering how caustically the founders examined the European political universe, it is curious that they still could not see how naive their hopes for America were. They expected the United States to be a new kind of society, partyless, where democracy spread magically because great thinkers representing the people wished it so.

Now, of course, we know differently, and evidence of opposition parties is one of the most important ways to measure the vital signs of an emerging democracy. Such parties normally appear well after a successful revolution, but they are no less crucial to the evolution of a civil society, as anyone from Zimbabwe, Cuba, or Hong Kong can confirm. Van Buren, while not a radical thinker, deserves full credit for realizing this truth ahead of his compatriots. It was a huge contribution, lost in the obscurity of the early republic, somewhere between the Erie Canal and the Tariff of Abominations, but more important than either. Not only is the spirit of party not hostile to democracy, it is essential to it. We are all familiar with the deficiencies of the two-party system—the acrimony, gridlock, and corruption that taint the process more than we care to admit. However, there is a fundamental balance at its core—an internal gyroscope, based on brute competition—that has allowed this system to continue, with only a few modifications, from 1828 to the present. That gyroscope was built by Van Buren, and every time we ask another country to replicate it, we are paying silent homage to him.

But even with all the hindsight that history can confer, it is unclear how exactly Van Buren wrought this great change. We know that he did it between about 1826 and 1828, and that Jackson's election in the latter year marks the beginning of what we now see as an important new epoch, one of those curious moments when the wind shifts and a new phase of human behavior begins. But it is no less evident that for all of Andrew Jackson's great charisma, Van Buren was a far deeper theorist on party issues and his vision was indispensable to the rise of the phenomenon we call Jacksonian Democracy.

How did Van Buren do it? Even at the time, contemporaries complained about what is now the historian's dilemma—that no one knows exactly what he was up to as he built his new party. But a thousand cat-steps brought him invisibly toward his destination. It was not always easy to see the traces, but year after year the structure rose, like a great Mayan temple, its progress slow if measured by days but irrefutable at the end of a decade.

Much of his progress was instinctive. If nothing else, Van Buren was a social creature. A widower, blond and charming, in control of thirty-six electoral votes, he was bound to be popular in the Washington scene. The Democratic Party may have begun, in fact, as a party—or at least an extension of the idea that like-minded people enjoy being together. From the moment of his arrival he was in the thick of it, playing cards with Calhoun's friends, talking horses with John Randolph of Roanoke, visiting congressmen and senators at their country seats, and loving every minute of his relevance. Even opponents paid tribute to his charm, saying that he was "a host in himself, the idol and pride of his party." He often retired to Saratoga during the racing season, and here the socializing continued, with Southern and Western allies coming great distances to confer with the great strategist. Pleasure and politics coincided nicely, and it is clear that part of Van Buren's success at building a national organization lay in his ability to entertain well. The Democratic Party has always been a movable feast.

In particular, Van Buren liked the ladies of Washington, flattering and cajoling them, gossiping about their husbands with them, making them laugh. He probably destroyed an extensive correspondence with his female confidantes (what is left is perfectly fine, but terribly official). One especially caught his eye—Ellen Randolph, the granddaughter of his hero Thomas Jefferson. The gossips had a field day when Ellen, by then a frequent consort, asked the band at a ball to play her favorite song—"The Yellow-Haired Laddie." Still, there is no evidence that Van Buren ever committed any indiscretions during his long career at the center of Washington society—he managed to combine perfectly the seeming capacity for sin with the refusal to commit it (a rare feat indeed).

As might be expected, these characteristics endeared him to the Southern politicians in Washington. Van Buren was a peculiar sort of Northerner—he was fun—and he would share a special rapport with the South throughout his career. He instinctively gravitated toward "bold" politicians of the "old school"—the original followers of Jefferson, now aging but still full of vinegar, and as alienated from Monroe as he. Van Buren took care to state his fidelity to the creed—government should be modest, banks in particular should be constrained, and internal improvements should be local and limited. The Supreme Court should be knocked back down to size, and anything else that was not spelled out by the Constitution should be prohibited. Soon, a host of influential Southerners— Nathaniel Macon, John Taylor, William Crawford, among others— were paying attention to the diminutive New Yorker.

To cultivate these friendships and advance the simultaneous goal of building the party through an expanding network of allies, Van Buren took frequent long trips into the Southland. It was the age of the tour—Lafayette's long pilgrimage across America had electrified the people in 1824–25—and Van Buren grasped sooner than most that traveling was another form of politicking. His journeys, early versions of the barnstorming tour, were deeply mysterious to the oracles of Washington, who could never quite determine what Van Buren was up to. According to one correspondent, opinion was divided as to whether he had traveled because of "a great plot to revive the republican party," or because of "a beautiful & accomplished lady, not distantly related to the Governor of Virginia, and that an alliance of portentous consequences was then to be formed between 'the ancient dominion' and this 'great state.'"

One of the most important friendships he made was with Thomas Ritchie, a leading editor and political thinker who had much of Virginia wrapped around his finger and ran the Richmond Junto the same way that Van Buren ran the Albany Regency. They met in the spring of 1823, and something clicked (fifteen years later, Ritchie wrote that from "the first moment of my acquaintance with you, I have been your personal & political friend."). As usual, Calhoun was one of the first to notice that the air had shifted: "Between the Regency at Albany and the junto at Richmond, there is a vital connection. They give and receive help from each other, and confidently expect to govern this nation." With the revival of the New York–Virginia alliance that had propelled Jefferson and Burr to power, and before that Washington and Hamilton, could anything stop them?

A year later Van Buren paid the most important visit of all: to the Sage of Monticello himself, the original partisan leader, still alive nearly fifty years after setting events in motion with the Declaration of Independence. Jefferson received him for several days in May 1824, and to Van Buren it was nothing less than a laying on of hands. Decades later, re-creating the event in his memoirs, the years melted away and he was with Jefferson again: "It may well be imagined with how much satisfaction I listened to Mr. Jefferson's conversation. His imposing appearance as he sat uncovered—never wearing his hat except when he left the carriage and often not then—and the earnest and impressive manner in which he spoke of men and things, are yet as fresh in my recollection as if they were experiences of yesterday." Van Buren left Monticello with a renewed sense of purpose, having found his "beau ideal." Jefferson confirmed his sense that Monroe was an apostate Jeffersonian (in a letter to Van Buren, he wrote, "Tories are Tories still, by whatever name they be called."). Van Buren wrote back to Jefferson, immodestly, that he hoped to personally rescue Jefferson's country "from misrule."

Washington society grew apprehensive at the news of this May-December frolic. An informant to Andrew Jackson, with whom Van Buren was not yet allied, wrote the general, "It seems that Mr. Van Buren, not content with the exercise of his talents for intrigue in his own state, must try his powers with the ancient Dominion." John Quincy Adams noted in his diary that Van Buren resembled Jefferson in "profound dissimulation and duplicity," but that he also reminded him of James Madison for his discretion and disinclination for open conflict. In fact, Van Buren would soon launch a correspondence with Madison as well. He made a surprising prilgrimage to Quincy, Massachusetts, to visit an ancient John Adams. The old masters were still alive; why not take their pulse now and then?

That same year, 1824, presented an important chance to develop these embryonic thoughts into a concrete course of action. Monroe was finally leaving office, and the presidency was up for grabs among an unusually large number of strong contenders, including Calhoun, Clay, Adams, Jackson, and Georgia's William H. Crawford, the crusty old Treasury secretary. Thanks to Monroe's vague policy of "fusion," there was no clear consensus, and an unusually bitter election followed. Van Buren felt his way forward in this complicated situation, and eventually settled on Crawford as the truest "democrat," to use the word that was beginning to see the light of day more and more frequently (it had a pejorative taint during the excesses of the French Revolution, but that was now ancient history). Despite their friendship, he was distressed by Calhoun's disdain for the caucus, which Van Buren considered the linchpin of the republican tradition, a crucial instrument for creating party policy and disciplining wafflers. The long schism between Calhoun and Van Buren, on and off again for so many years, probably originated

in this minor dispute. Amazingly, given later events, Calhoun criticized Van Buren in 1823 for a dangerous radicalism that gave too
much emphasis to states' rights.

In February 1824, Van Buren convened just such a caucus to
coax his selection forward and verify that the party would go
along—even though in this case "the party" barely existed. At a rump
meeting, a caucus of congressmen and senators confirmed the selection of Crawford. In many ways, the nomination was more important than the nominee, because it signaled an emerging coalition of
Northerners and Southerners, opposed to the quasi-Federalism of
the administration and guided by Van Buren and Thomas Ritchie,
pulling levers in the nation's two most important states.

That does not mean there were not big challenges to the Crawford team. An impressive setback occurred even before the nomination, when Crawford suffered a paralytic stroke that left him
largely unable to speak, see, or move (a perfect candidate for a kingmaker like Van Buren). He recovered to an extent, but not sufficiently to run or serve, and the fact that Van Buren pushed the
doomed campaign as far as he did does not reflect especially well
on his record. In fact, Crawford was likely the sickest man ever to
run for president, more infirm than Franklin Roosevelt in 1944.

Van Buren also had other problems on his plate, especially back
home in New York, where the Regency was not running itself as
well as usual. Some of it was his fault. To strengthen Crawford's
chances, he decided that it was necessary for the Regency to reject a
popular drive to vote directly for presidential electors—a miscalcu-
lation that flew in the face of his general sympathy for extending
the suffrage and hurt his party in New York.

To make matters worse, an underling had stupidly removed De
Witt Clinton from the board that oversaw the Erie Canal, a move
that backfired and aroused public sympathy for Clinton, resulting
in Clinton's reelection as governor (Van Buren exploded, "There is
such a thing in politics as killing a man too dead!"). After hearing
the results from New York ("a tornado"), he complained that he

was "as completely broken down a politician as my bitterest enemies could desire."

The results in Washington were just as depressing. Despite a
long, drawn-out process of choosing the next president, which he
thought he could influence at several crucial stages in Congress, the
House of Representatives ultimately awarded the 1824 election to
John Quincy Adams, thanks to some adroit politicking by Henry
Clay. One of Adams's supporters exulted that Van Buren looked
like "a wilted cabbage" after getting the news. He had backed the
wrong man, had stuck with him for far too long, and had lost further prestige by failing to stop the election of Adams in Congress.

But Van Buren could not stay down for long, not as long as his
fortunes were tied to New York's. In all of American history, it
would be hard to find a state that rose more rapidly than New York
in the early decades of the nineteenth century. The Erie Canal was
completed in 1825, but even before, there was rapidly mounting
evidence of New York's extraordinary growth. In 1790, Virginia was
the most populous state by far, with 692,000 people, twice as many
as New York; by 1820, New York was first, with over a million. In
1825, New York's customs receipts constituted almost $16 million
toward the national figure of $27 million. Virginia, at the same
time, was losing wealth precipitously; between 1817 and 1829 its
land values dropped from $206 million to $96 million. It seemed
time to recalibrate the political value of the two states as well. One
of Van Buren's lieutenants wrote, "My only solicitude is that these
consummate braggadocios from Virginia may be put down." Van
Buren may have liked the South, but there is no doubt that he, too,
sought a greater influence for the Empire State.

Despite the catastrophe of the Crawford candidacy, the pieces
were in place for another, far better organized effort in 1828. To
restore his damaged credibility, Van Buren had to begin by mending
fences at home. That meant a rapprochement with his old adversary De Witt Clinton. They agreed to make life a little more toler-
able for each other, and Van Buren bought himself a little time to

plan his next moves. Jabez Hammond, the chronicler of New York politics, called their dalliance a "backstairs intercourse," and what that phrase lacks in poetry it makes up for in vividness. Without Clinton dogging him every step of the way, Van Buren's reelection to the Senate in 1827 was easier. Their détente also facilitated a new chess move of the highest importance: the gradual alignment of the proto-party Van Buren had formed in 1824 behind the most attractive candidate of them all, Andrew Jackson. Clinton's early support for Jackson had delayed Van Buren's embrace of Old Hickory, along with some concern over Jackson's willingness to embrace pure Jeffersonian ideals. But now all that changed, and Jackson's group of friends converged with the impressive organization Van Buren had built. With a worthy actor enlisted for the starring role, Van Buren agreed to direct, produce, and even build the stage.

In one specific sense, the disaster of 1824 brought a great gift to Van Buren. He could hardly have asked for a president who more eerily conjured the ghosts of Federalism than John Quincy Adams, who not only resembled his father physically, but retained his choleric intolerance for the little gestures that oil the machine works of American politics. For all his remarkable talents, Adams was in many ways a maladroit politician, and his heavy-handed nationalism fit perfectly into Van Buren's plans to define a new and pure Republicanism. The so-called corrupt bargain, by which Clay engineered Adams's election in the House in return for a high position (secretary of state), inflamed further opposition, and the Virginia firebrand John Randolph excoriated "the puritan and the blackleg" for their marriage of convenience. Adams's patronage policies exacerbated the prevailing distrust in the air, for he hired former Federalists along with Republicans (Van Buren complained that Adams did not care if his support came from "Jew or Gentile"). What had been a vague restlessness under Monroe now burst forth as a full-fledged opposition party, with Van Buren calling the shots.

Some of these developments took place in the public eye, in the halls of Congress, where Van Buren and his friends began to oppose the policies of the Adams administration. Many of these policies seem quite reasonable in hindsight (a diplomatic mission to a pan-American Congress in Panama, federal support for national education, expanded internal improvements), but they exacerbated the prevailing sense that crypto-Federalists had seized control of the government, and they fed the voracious creature Van Buren was raising.

But as usual, many of Van Buren's best moves took place far from the public eye. Like a nineteenth-century Vito Corleone, he was always thinking ahead of his enemies, forging a new network of families and alliances that would forever redraw the map of power in the United States. Everything he did contributed to the goal of unfurling a new national party, nominally Jeffersonian but now hitched to the rising star of Andrew Jackson. On vacation in Saratoga in the summer of 1826, he entertained visitors from the North, South, and West, and fine-tuned the plan. Young Charles Francis Adams, the president's puritanical son, denounced Saratoga as a place devoted only to pleasure, with "riding, singing, drinking, dancing . . . the constant order of the day and night." It was exactly the kind of place where Van Buren did his best work, and here he began to cobble together the disparate subparties of Jackson, Calhoun, and Crawford. He also continued his mysterious journeys deep into the heartland to forge strategic friendships. He scored a coup over the Christmas holidays in 1826 when he traveled to South Carolina and secured Calhoun's acquiescence (this despite the fact that Calhoun was Adams's vice president). He and Calhoun had already arranged for a new opposition newspaper in Washington, and when the Senate steered its lucrative printing jobs toward this paper, no one needed to ask who was behind it. Van Buren also found other regional power brokers besides Thomas Ritchie, including Isaac Hill of New Hampshire, Amos Kendall and Francis Blair of Kentucky, James Buchanan of Pennsylvania, Thomas Hart Benton of Missouri, and the clique of Jackson supporters around Nashville. A national network of politicians and journalists acting in concert, vastly larger and more modern than Jefferson's Republican Party, was ready to unleash its energies.

Van Buren usually covered his tracks well, but fortunately we have one piece of vivid evidence that testifies to Van Buren's role in these seismic events. On January 13, 1827, Van Buren wrote a letter to Thomas Ritchie that outlined his grandiose hopes for the organization they were building. He began by describing the desirability of a national convention to present their candidate to the world, which would in turn lead to "the substantial reorganization of the Old Republican Party." The new organization, "the democracy," would "draw anew the old Party lines" and bring better organization to the sloppy system of presidential nomination, which revolved too much around personalities and not enough around principles (the same argument he had made against De Witt Clinton). He added a point that the Virginian could not have failed to appreciate: the creation of national parties would soften sectional tension over slavery.

In other words, Van Buren was making an offer that Ritchie could not refuse: if Virginia would yoke itself to New York in a new system, they would prevail against all opponents, and avoid the far worse specter of Virginia's growing economic and political irrelevance. Without saying it, Van Buren was implying that Virginia would be the junior partner and that the Virginia dynasty was now a thing of the past, but that Virginia would be protected by a senior partner that kept the slavery issue from getting out of hand. With the right candidate now on board, there was little they could not do. Van Buren understood that he was ushering in a new era: "the effect of such a nomination of Gen'l Jackson could not fail to be considerable. His election, as the result of his military services without reference to party & so far as he alone is concerned, scarcely to principle, would be one thing. His election as the result of a combined and concerted effort of a political party, holding in the main to certain tenets & opposed to certain prevailing principles, might be another and a far different thing." Three months later, Ritchie accepted the proposal. The different thing, the Democracy, was born.

Obviously, the growth of a large political machine, whirring and clanking across the Union, could be concealed for only so long. Opponents struggled for the right vocabulary to describe the entity that was coming into existence. The *National Intelligencer*, an influential newspaper, shrilly denounced these intrigues to create a "Central Junta" at the head of a new "cabbalistic organization." Rush Limbaugh could hardly have said it better. In South Carolina, one wit wrote a fake advertisement: "Martin Van Buren, Cabinet maker and Joiner, No. 1 Albany street, New York, informs his friends and the public that he has with great labour and sagacity succeeded in the composition of a new Panacea" to treat "the most difficult disorders . . . in the system of political men." Van Buren was either vilified or celebrated as the "Master Spirit" behind these changes, the "life and soul" of the movement, and inevitably as the "magician" who was ensorcelling influential leaders around the country. As the machine grew larger, its mechanic-in-chief loomed larger in the imaginations of his opponents, until Van Buren began to resemble one of the vaguely sinister scientists who populate so many gothic tales of the period.

None of this activity was lost on President Adams, who could not have looked upon Van Buren's activity with more disfavor if he was an emissary from the Vatican seeking to convert Yankee maids to Papism and then sell them into white slavery. In one of his most vituperative journal entries, he managed to disembowel Van Buren for reasons ranging from his parentage to his politics to Aaron Burr's treason (the Adamses were nothing if not efficient—why write only one insult when three would get you so much more for your ink expenditure?).

Van Buren is now the great electioneering manager for General Jackson, as he was before the last election for Mr. Crawford. He is now acting over the part in the affairs of the Union which Aaron Burr performed in 1799 and 1800; and there is much resemblance of character, manners, and even person between the two men. Van Buren, however, has improved as much in the art of electioneering upon Burr as the State of New York has grown in relative strength and importance in the Union. Van Buren has now every prospect of success in his present movements, and he will avoid the rock upon which Burr afterwards split.

That was a prescient observation, and mixed some admiration with a generous dose of New England cynicism. In truth, Van Buren deserved the credit Adams gave him. The creation of the Democratic Party was the achievement of a lifetime, and too many biographers pass over these years to get to his presidency. If he had never been elected, he still would have been important for his guerrilla activity in the middle of the 1820s. He defeated more than an administration; he destroyed an entire system that had ossified and installed in its place something far more modern.

Van Buren's work was now nearly complete. Within the space of two short years, from roughly 1826 to 1828, he had built a political organization that would dominate American government until the Civil War, and would survive that conflict to become one of the two major parties of the twentieth century. We will never know exactly what he did, step by step, but whatever it was should be taught in business school. For the creation of the Democratic Party was an accomplishment worthy of the great economic empires that were under construction around North America at the same time: the Astor fur and real estate concerns, the mercantile firms swelling coffers in coastal cities, the textile factories churning out broadcloth in New England river valleys, and the enormous companies coming into existence to manage the raw materials coming out of the American West.

Of course, he still had to win the 1828 election, and that meant deepening his relationship with the candidate at the top of the pyramid he was building. At first, Jackson and Van Buren were wary of each other—respectful, but hardly intimate. They had served in the Senate together, and each admired the other's activities during the crucible of the second war against the British. But they were very different men, each a little suspicious of the other. Van Buren's reputation as a magician preceded him wherever he went, and Jackson had not exactly shown fidelity to Jefferson's original principles during his early political career. Yet there was much to unite them: a disdain for the Adams-Clay coalition, a visceral sense that wealthy interests should not receive special privileges, and, more than anything, a fierce desire to win. There was something else as well that may or may not have come up in private conversations, far from prying eyes: each had undergone, early in his career, a dangerous fascination with Aaron Burr. To this day we still do not know how close young Andrew Jackson came to throwing his lot in with Burr's efforts to create an American empire outside the jurisdiction of the United States. Van Buren, one suspects, could relate to the spell that had hypnotized his candidate twenty years earlier.

They drew closer as the election neared. In the fall of 1827, Van Buren wrote two interesting letters to Jackson, offering advice the way a parent would to a child (in fact Jackson was fifteen years older), urging him to leave the politics to the professionals and merely to appear presidential. It was not the last time that advice would be offered to a presidential candidate. But the letters grew longer in 1828. And their friendship deepened after the shocking death of De Witt Clinton in February. It had been mildly awkward that the old rivals Clinton and Van Buren were both in the Jackson camp. Now that Clinton was gone, it fell to Van Buren alone to deliver the Empire State, and with it the presidency. Van Buren delivered a moving eulogy to Clinton, perhaps the best speech he ever gave. Jackson's great nineteenth-century biographer James Parton wrote that Clinton's removal from the scene left Van Buren with a hand "full of cards," all of them trumps.

But politics never stops, and there were still a few thorny issues to work out before the election. One of the most sensitive was the tariff question—a matter that bitterly separated Northerners and Southerners, presaging in some ways the Civil War, though it was not ostensibly about slavery on the surface. A South Carolinian supporter wrote Van Buren that he was "treading on the crest of a lava not yet solid." In December 1827 the Jackson coalition took over Congress, and Van Buren was forced to stare squarely at the problem. Through his reliable friend Silas Wright, he orchestrated a new tariff that spread benefits to different groups and brought together politicians representing Northern farmers and Southerners. Though deplored as the "tariff of abominations" by its opponents, particularly by Northern manufacturers who felt it gave too little protection, the tariff was an impressive example of Van Buren's competence as a political manager and gave encouraging evidence that the Jacksonians would be a legislative force as well as a presidential party.

In the spring of 1828, as the presidential excitement was heating up, Van Buren received pressure from his friends in Albany to return and run for governor of New York. It seems counterintuitive to a modern audience—why would he return to Albany? But as a hardened political operative, he could see the logic—his campaign would help ensure that New York went for Jackson, and it would shore up Van Buren's credentials as an electable successor to the elderly general he was trying to install in the White House.

He decided to do it—and after he sold his Washington furniture at auction, it was noticed that the carpet was threadbare in front of his mirror, from the thousands of times he had rehearsed his speeches to himself.

Some of the glimpses we get of Van Buren during this campaign are markedly different from the staid figure who stares at us from his official portraits. As he canvassed the counties of western New York, he was resplendent in his outrageously colorful costume, dazzling voters with an outfit that showed how far he had come from Kinderhook. A pious churchgoer never forgot the impression: "His complexion was bright blond and he dressed accordingly. On this occasion he wore an elegant snuff-colored broadcloth coat, with velvet collar to match; his cravat was orange tinted silk with modest lace tips; his vest was of pearl hue; his trousers were white duck; his silk hose corresponded to his vest, his shoes were Morocco; his nicely fitting gloves were yellow kid; his hat, a long-furred beaver, with broad brim, was of Quaker color." Van Buren planned a campaign for Jackson that was no less uproarious, and across the Union there were deafening parades, gaudy souvenirs, and drunken songs without end. The dour Adams never had a chance.

The election offered a sweet reward for all the long years Van Buren had put into his cause. Jackson won by a huge margin, drawing support in every region except New England. Van Buren, too, was easily elected as governor. In his inaugural address, delivered in January 1829, he showered unusual attention on the new kinds of modern problems that were beginning to afflict New Yorkers—urban problems like juvenile delinquency, economic problems like bank regulation, and election reform. Nearly exactly a century later, in the same place, Franklin D. Roosevelt would inaugurate his gubernatorial career with another policy-driven address.

Yet Van Buren would not remain governor for long. As Jackson formed his cabinet, it was obvious that he would consult with the adviser who had done so much for him. A month later, Jackson offered him the most prestigious position that was in his power to give: secretary of state. Van Buren was hardly an expert in international affairs, and some of his most strident speeches against John Quincy Adams and Henry Clay had deployed a rather cheap isolationism against their administration. But there was far more to the position than an interest in the rest of the world, as anyone knew who lived in Washington. It offered the chance to continue at Jackson's side, eminent beyond all others, and ultimately to compete for the presidency himself, after the single term that Jackson claimed he would serve. Or perhaps it would be more accurate to say, eminent beyond every other save one, for Vice President Calhoun (under Adams) had now become Vice President Calhoun (under Jackson)—the only time a vice president has succeeded himself under a different president. Both Calhoun and Van Buren had contributed mightily to the new alliance in power. But there were dark premonitions, as there always are with incoming administrations, far beneath the exuberance at the surface. James Buchanan wrote, "Disguise it as we may, the friends of Van Buren and those of Calhoun are becoming very jealous of each other."

Still, he had so much to feel proud of on the day that Jackson was inaugurated in March 1829, one of the great days in the history of participatory democracy. A tidal wave of humanity (twenty thousand strong) poured into Washington, eager to see the coronation of their champion, already called "the people's president." Some were exhilarated, but others likened the inaugural to "the inundation of the northern barbarians into Rome." A society matron was horrified when she attended the reception at the White House, only to find "a rabble, a mob, of boys, negros, women, children, scrambling, fighting, romping." Jackson himself was "nearly pressed to death" by the frenzy of adulation and barely escaped to a nearby hotel. A fourteen-hundred-pound cheese sent by an admirer in New York was not only devoured by the rabble but so completely stomped into the carpets of the White House that the stench lingered for weeks. Van Buren could not have asked for a more dramatic way to announce the new age. As his friend James Hamilton, Alexander's son, wrote him, "Notwithstanding the row Demos kicked up, the whole matter went off very well."

Did Van Buren understand the full force of the power he had unleashed? A private notebook entry gives a clue:

Those who have wrought great changes in the world never succeeded by gaining over chiefs; but always by exciting the multitude. The first is the resource of intrigue and produces only secondary results, the second is the resort of genius and transforms the universe.

4

———

Ascendancy

It was a time for new beginnings and, paradoxically, a time of deep nostalgia for the past. In 1828, when the first major railroad in the United States, the Baltimore and Ohio, launched its service, an ancient signer of the Declaration of Independence, Charles Carroll, was incongruously on hand to celebrate the advent of an age very different from his own. Likewise, Andrew Jackson was a peculiar choice to lead what was, in more ways than one, a political youth movement. At sixty-one, he was the oldest man to have been elected president. But he, too, had experienced the American Revolution firsthand (as several gruesome scars testified), and the crotchety old general was the perfect symbol for the unwieldy group of outsiders and backbenchers that had united around him to form the new Democratic Party.

It is rather odd that the party's architect was not there for Jackson's riotous inaugural on March 4, having spent the better part of a decade planning for the day. But Governor Van Buren still had business to attend to in New York, and he did not come to the capital until March 22. For all the excitement he felt, there were already clouds on the horizon. Factions were forming in the new government (a friend wrote, "If I went into the Cabinet I would cut my throat"), and jealous office-seekers dogged Van Buren's steps everywhere he went. He arrived in Washington after dark, only to find a horde of job applicants filling his hotel room. After an arduous hour entertaining their requests, he ventured to the White House to present his respects to the new president. Despite all that they had done together, this was the first time Jackson and Van Buren had met in person since forming their alliance. More than two decades later, Van Buren remembered the moment vividly and gave his tedious memoir more life than usual: "A solitary lamp in the vestibule and a single candle in the President's office gave no promise of the cordiality with which I was, notwithstanding, greeted by General Jackson on my visit to the White House." Jackson, although unhealthy and depressed by his wife's recent death, greeted his exhausted visitor with a warmth he was not expecting. It was the beginning of a most unusual political friendship, and "from that night to the day of his death the relations, sometimes official, always political and personal, were inviolably maintained between that noble old man and myself, the cordial and confidential character of which can never have been surpassed among public men."

They had their work cut out for them. Each had scored a great personal triumph—Jackson in finally achieving the presidency, Van Buren in building the platform for him to stand on. But it was one thing to form an opposition; it was quite another to govern. And in the act of opposing, they had of course created a few opponents of their own. Again, the Regency offered a model of how to move forward and consolidate the gains they had made—through patronage, press, and close liaisons with Congress.

Over time, the Jacksonians would excel in all three areas. The number of federal employees roughly doubled, to sixty thousand, and a huge number of sympathetic officeholders were brought in (a Regency lieutenant, William Marcy, had won both critics and admirers for stating honestly, "To the victor belong the spoils"). But it was rough going at first. Van Buren, who prided himself in his sensitive handling of appointments, was hurt by a number of early blunders that were made without his input, including inappropriate appointments in New York and in the foreign service, both technically under his supervision. One night he walked the streets of Washington "until a late hour," wondering whether to submit his resignation as secretary of state the next day. He was also put off by the number of strong personalities clustered around Jackson, each expecting attention and influence. The Democratic Party, still in its infancy, was a stool with three legs. There were Westerners that Jackson had brought in, Southerners under the sway of Calhoun, and Old School Jeffersonians around Van Buren, including Virginians and New Yorkers. But no group had a monopoly, and that only exacerbated the jockeying for position. Over time, a small, core group of advisers would emerge, including at various times Van Buren, John Eaton, Amos Kendall, and Francis Preston Blair. This Kitchen Cabinet, as it was called, would prove to be a great comfort to Jackson, but it took time to coalesce.

Calhoun presented a particularly thorny problem. To this day, it's intimidating even to stare at a daguerreotype of the fierce South Carolinian. Imagine what it was like to become the focal point of his wrath. For nearly a decade, since the day he welcomed Van Buren to Washington, he had watched the New Yorker creep up on him. It was insulting enough that Van Buren had torpedoed his chances for the presidency in 1824, when Calhoun was the rising star of a new generation; now Van Buren was a rival in his own right. Any sapient student of American economic trends—as Calhoun surely was—could tell that New York's strength was increasing with the Erie Canal, and that the South would lose influence if special measures were not taken to protect it. For each of these reasons, Calhoun reorganized his priorities as the Jacksonians came to power. The former nationalist became an ardent sectional champion, responding to the Tariff of Abominations in 1828 ("northern perfidy") with his *Exposition and Protest*, which advanced the dangerous idea that a state could nullify any federal law it disliked. And the once-generous politician became extraordinarily sensitive to

Van Buren's rise and to the problem that simmered below the surface of their enmity—slavery. It was the beginning of a long slide—
what often happens to powerful Washington insiders who believe
they should be president.

Despite the early slights, Van Buren wisely kept his counsel, and
his friendship with Jackson grew incrementally from the moment
of his arrival. To this day, one wonders a little: Who was using
whom? Yet they seem to have felt genuine affection for each other,
and for long stretches of his presidency Jackson valued Van Buren's
advice above all others'. Van Buren's enemies were driven to dis-
traction by their obvious closeness. John Quincy Adams destested
their "political love-potions." Davy Crockett wrote, with his usual
bluntness, "Van Buren is as opposite to Jackson as dung is to a dia-
mond."

One reason for their friendship is precisely the fact that they were
so different. Like connecting pieces of a jigsaw puzzle, each offered
something the other lacked. Jackson, famously short-tempered, did
not always foresee the long-term consequences of his tantrums.
There was something terrifying about his anger, and more than a
few widows in Tennessee regretted that their late husbands had
made disparaging remarks within his earshot. Jefferson once wrote,
"When I was President of the Senate and he was a Senator, he could
never speak on account of the rashness of his feelings. I have seen
him attempt it repeatedly and as often choke with rage."

The Careful Dutchman, on the other hand, was a natural concil-
iator, and a gifted strategist who could convert Jackson's pathological urges into meaningful policy. He also made Jackson laugh, and
the president was convinced that his favorite newspaper humorist
was secretly Van Buren. Before long, they had grown close, and Van
Buren was spending considerable time at the White House, eating,
drinking, and even, according to one source, playing blindman's
bluff with the children of Jackson's secretary. He was described as
the president's "constant riding, walking and visiting companion,"
and Jackson went out of his way to defend Van Buren from the

usual charges that he was an intriguer. Jackson, who detested guile and deception above all other things, claimed that Van Buren was "one of the most frank men" he knew—"a true man with no guile." Either Van Buren's enemies exaggerated his slyness, or he was very sharp indeed.

For all their differences, they shared some important common traits. Neither was to the manor born, and the fact that Van Buren had been attacked so often in the press created a certain bond. Jackson had been through a searing experience in the 1828 campaign, denounced as a murderer and adulterer, and he was convinced that the death of his beloved wife, Rachel, stemmed from the attacks. Furthermore, both were widowers in a town where that meant something. Since Dolley Madison's benign rule over Washington in the teens, a formidable force had been gathering strength in the capital—the influence of political wives. Nearly as soon as the British retreated, they advanced, and in the 1820s, as Washington became less an architectural sketch and more a genuine community, it was inevitable that these powerful spouses would feel their growing power over the destinies of the young republic. And they would advance their power through what passed for weapons of mass destruction at the time: gossip, innuendo, and outright slander. The historian Robert Darnton has brilliantly explored the power of gossip in pre-Revolutionary France—how pornographic bagatelles concerning Marie Antoinette eroded confidence in the monarchy, and whispered half-truths pitted rival factions against one another in court circles. Mud-soaked Washington was a long distance from Versailles, but the same eternal principles held. In one of the most memorable lines that he ever put on paper, Van Buren wrote, "You might as well turn the current of the Niagara with a ladies fan as to prevent scheming & intrigue at Washington."

All of these trends—the excitement of a new administration, the instability of the coalition, the Van Buren–Calhoun rivalry, Jackson's temper, and the growing power of gossip—combined to lay the groundwork for the mother of all sex scandals, the Peggy Eaton affair. Has there ever been one that was not at heart political? Washington has a long history of high moral excitements—great upheavals that, once a generation or so, inflame the local rumor-mongers before they settle back into the Jurassic ooze of everyday social life. One thinks a little of Wilbur Mills, or Gary Hart, or the Lewinsky crisis, with its air of hyperbolic righteousness, and the swirling political currents secretly propelling events at the surface. Seemingly about nothing at first, the Eaton affair combined sex and politics to force a decisive power shift within the cabinet—in exactly the opposite direction than was intended.

Peggy Eaton, the wife of Jackson's close friend and secretary of war, John Eaton, had a long history of her own. She had grown up in the district—a claim not many could then make—as Peggy O'Neale, an attractive girl rising to maturity before all the world in her father's boardinghouse. After having a few affairs (the precise number was in dispute), she married a young sailor when she was sixteen, but during his long absences she fell back into her old habits. Soon she was committing adultery with Eaton, then a prominent senator. After her husband died, she and Eaton were married at the beginning of 1829, just as the administration was forming. It was the talk of Washington society, and a friend of Van Buren's wrote him in rapture, comparing Eaton's ill-advised marriage to the act of using a chamber pot and then accidentally putting it on one's head.

This would hardly seem like a scandal worthy of the name today. No one was caught in flagrante delicto, and for all the negative attention they received, John and Peggy Eaton appear to have loved each other. Their beautiful town house lasted until the 1950s, when it was the Capitol Hill Club, exactly the kind of conservative bastion that their accusers would have felt comfortable in. But their timing in 1829 could not have been worse. Washington was not ready to accept a woman with Peggy's past as a prominent political hostess (her crime may have been her low upbringing rather than her sexual indiscretion). As soon as the new administration began, a clique of cabinet wives, led by Calhoun's, publicly snubbed Mrs. Eaton, refusing to visit her or to acknowledge her existence in any way.

Jackson responded as one might expect: he completely flew off the handle. Reminded of the partisan attacks on his own wife (whose marriage to him overlooked a few legal niceties), Jackson took umbrage on behalf of Peggy Eaton and was soon utterly consumed by what Van Buren dubbed "the Eaton malaria." Memorably, he said, "I had rather have live vermin on my back than the tongue of one of these Washington women on my reputation."

We will never know exactly what motivated Van Buren to defend Peggy—it could have been his acute nose for political advantage, or the fact that he had no wife, or maybe just his innate sense of justice. He knew a little about growing up in a tavern and having proper people look down on you—and must have instinctively responded to a logic that appears in her memoir: "I am not ashamed to say that I was born in the Franklin House and that my father was a tavern-keeper. I have always been superior to that petty American foolery." Around the same time, his wealthy New York enemies were having a field day with the discovery of a letter Van Buren had written in which he complained, "My suffering is intolerable." In any event, Van Buren did not merely tolerate her—he actively cultivated her friendship. This was hardly the act of a conniving schemer—it was a risky decision in an unforgiving political climate, and he did it in style, calling on Peggy as soon as he arrived in Washington. A remarkable sentence from a nineteenth-century historian conveys the drama of that first visit—a visit that reordered the cabinet and ultimately gave Van Buren the presidency: "The political history of the last thirty years, dates from the moment when the soft hand of Mr. Van Buren touched Mrs. Eaton's knocker."

We can laugh at the melodramatic writing, but something rings true about that grandiose claim. Jackson never forgave Calhoun for his role in the Eaton affair, and never forgot his gratitude to

Van Buren. The crisis brought out his best qualities, and John
Quincy Adams recorded that the cabinet was badly divided
between Calhoun, leading the "moral party," and Van Buren leading
the "frail sisterhood." One could even argue that the Civil War
sprang from Peggy Eaton's peccadilloes—for Calhoun's rage at Van
Buren was just the beginning of a lifelong mania against Northern
political power, and each crisis between 1828 and 1860 seemed to
spring from the one immediately preceding it. In a sense, it's all one
story, and secession arguably resulted from succession—or, specifically, Calhoun's failure to succeed Jackson. As early as December
1829, less than a year after taking office, Jackson had already privately designated Van Buren as his successor in an emergency.

Part of the reason for this evolving trust was Van Buren's successful administration of the State Department. Clearly, he enjoyed
his new job for the simple fact that it was important. Friends predicted that he would divide his time between "international law
and the ladies." Unsurprisingly, this flattering smooth-talker was
good at diplomacy, and before long he had resolved two major
problems favorably, winning reciprocal trade benefits from the
United Kingdom in the West Indies and securing a large payment of
25 million francs from France for indemnities dating back to
Napoleon. He also successfully concluded the first treaty with the
Ottoman Empire—an important agreement that laid the foundation for the modern alliance between the United States and Turkey.
A visitor to the State Department left a florid description of Van
Buren during this period: "a bald-headed, but whiskered little gentleman, dressed in the extreme of fashion, full of smirks and smiles,
soft as the 'sweet South, breathing o'er violets,'—but penetrating as
a mercurial bath, or the poison of Upas."

Van Buren was also providing expert counsel to Jackson on a
wide range of other matters. Most famously, he drafted an early version of Jackson's Maysville Road veto, an important statement of
just how far the federal government should go to support the internal improvements endlessly under construction in the booming

United States. In a nutshell, he thought that truly federal projects—roads that stretched through many states—should be supported, but that local projects should be paid for locally. It was an important clarification of a murky issue, and smart politics as well, pleasing advocates on both sides of the issue.

Calhoun, meanwhile, was growing more and more frustrated with his seemingly endless vice presidency. As he sensed Van Buren's growing closeness to Jackson, an inner sense of physics pushed him away from both of them, and he began plotting his and South Carolina's revenge. There was always an innate tension at the heart of Jacksonian democracy—between the old-school republicanism of Van Buren's allies and the inchoate nationalism felt by Jackson. Nearly every major issue of the Jackson presidency touched on this fault line and forced Van Buren to find the middle ground he was so gifted at locating—keeping the government simple enough to please the Jeffersonian backers, but allowing the nation to grow fast enough to please Westerners and Northerners.

In 1830, after the arguments over the Tariff of Abominations and the Eaton affair, Calhoun was ready to apply more pressure. That year saw the legendary Senate debate between Calhoun's proxy, Robert Hayne, and Daniel Webster of Massachusetts, a debate in which Webster forcefully asserted the primacy of the federal government over the states. In the near aftermath, a Jefferson Day dinner was proposed for April 13 at Brown's Indian Queen Hotel in Washington, organized by Hayne. The planners innocently claimed that they wanted to bring Southern and Western Democrats together, but the dinner aroused Van Buren's suspicions that Calhoun was plotting to undermine the party by spreading nullification. In this charged climate, Jackson and Van Buren decided to make a stand, and they planned a suitable response.

Long-winded political dinners have been held in the capital since the dawn of the republic, but this one was truly memorable. At ten o'clock, after enduring dozens of toasts to Jefferson, Jackson stood up stiffly and raised his glass, staring fiercely at his vice president.

With six words, he shattered the ambience that Calhoun had created: "Our Union: It must be preserved." According to one observer, Calhoun's glass "trembled in his hand" and "a little of the amber fluid trickled down the side." Calhoun regained his composure, then spoke again in the code language that they both understood: "The Union—next to our liberty most dear." At that moment of high drama, Van Buren offered the kind of conciliatory toast he was best at: "Mutual forbearance and reciprocal concessions: thro' their agency the Union was established—the patriotic spirit from which they emanated will forever sustain it." The three toasts would never be forgotten by anyone who attended the dinner, and rightly so. Calhoun was preparing to declare a kind of independence from the United States, and Jackson told him that the United States would not tolerate it. Van Buren's friend Senator Thomas Hart Benton of Missouri later concluded that the dinner was nothing less than a plot "to dissolve the Union." Three decades later, Abraham Lincoln would remember the toasts well when he prepared to stand fast against South Carolina's secession.

From the dinner, things only got worse for Calhoun. His next disaster came courtesy of William Crawford, the Georgian whom Van Buren had supported for president in 1824. Crawford never liked Calhoun and now wanted Jackson to know what the president already suspected. Twelve years earlier, in 1818, when Calhoun was secretary of war, he wanted to arrest and try Jackson for his bloody and almost certainly extralegal raids into Florida. Jackson and Calhoun now took their gloves off. Jackson accused Calhoun of "duplicity and insincerity." Calhoun, in turn, published a scathing attack on Van Buren in the Washington newspaper he controlled. A paper loyal to Van Buren attacked Calhoun in return. The party was badly divided, and, despite all that he had done to cultivate the South throughout his career, Van Buren could now hear rumblings of discontent from below the Mason-Dixon Line.

Though Van Buren had won the early rounds, the toxicity of the atmosphere bothered him, and he knew as well as anyone that status can change very quickly in Washington. As he wrestled with the problem, he conceived a plan that would lead to a new cabinet and preserve his hopes to succeed Jackson someday. Van Buren offered to resign, giving Jackson an opening to ask for the resignations of other cabinet members as well, including John Eaton, who had already caused so much unwitting damage, and several of Calhoun's stooges. At first, Jackson recoiled from the plan, preferring as usual to meet all difficulties with stubborn resistance. But Van Buren wore him down, and ultimately he agreed. In gratitude, he named Van Buren to a post that he was sure to enjoy—minister to England. Calhoun presciently observed, with a mixture of jealousy and respect, that Van Buren had gained power while surrendering authority.

Van Buren sailed for England on August 16, 1831, happy to enjoy "the quietude of a midsummer Ocean" after twenty years of unceasing political infighting. Each day carried him "further from the sight and the sound of the political strife," and toward a position that he seemed to regard as part president-in-waiting, part Thomas Cook package tour. He was paid generously and was given a huge living expense, which he used to the last shilling. "Money—money is the thing," he wrote in an early and accurate diplomatic assessment he sent back home. Like Joseph Kennedy a century later, his relatively precarious origins in America did not stop him for a second from enjoying all that English society had to offer. From the moment he arrived, he felt at home. He and his charismatic son John, acting as his assistant, met all the luminaries of London, including the royal family, who took a fancy to him. One friendship, in particular, diverted him—Washington Irving was the secretary of the American legation, and he was only too happy to squire the new minister and his son around the historic sights, liberally enjoying "old English hospitality," probably a euphemism for the extraordinary variety of ales and beers that still greet travelers. They participated in a number of pagan Christmas revels—wassail bowls, mummers, boar's heads, and the like, and Irving wrote, "The more I see of Mr. V.B. the more I feel confirmed in a strong personal regard for him. He is one of the gentlest and most amiable men I have ever met with." Another evening Van Buren met the wily old French survivor Talleyrand, and they instinctively liked each other—one wishes their conversations could have been transcribed for the ages.

But after a few months of these heavy responsibilities, Calhoun caught up to him. In February, as the Queen was holding her first drawing room of the season, word reached London that the Senate had rejected Van Buren's appointment. Webster, Clay, and Calhoun, each with enough private reasons to thwart Van Buren's career, had combined to deal the blow—and Calhoun had gleefully cast the deciding vote as president of the Senate. "It will kill him, sir, kill him dead," he exulted to Thomas Hart Benton. Benton more accurately replied that Calhoun had "broken a minister," but "elected a Vice-President." The same boomerang effect that Van Buren had seen when the Regency fired De Witt Clinton was about to happen again, this time to his benefit. Reaction around the country was swift, and for nearly the first time in his life, Van Buren inspired a torrent of sympathetic outcries. Of course, he had not foreseen it—even Talleyrand could not have planned it this well—but there was no doubt that he was returning home with the enhanced status of a martyr, just as Jackson was casting about for a new vice president.

Before returning home, Van Buren took care of some old family business, visiting the Netherlands to investigate his roots and contemplate the miracle of social possibility that America had wrought for his peasant ancestors—ancestors who did not even have a proper last name when they first slouched toward the New World. Now, everywhere he went, he was a returning hero, the champion of international Dutchness and, some whispered, the future president of the United States. A very large step toward that end was taken back home, in Baltimore, when the first Democratic convention nominated Van Buren to replace Calhoun as Jackson's vice president for the second term Jackson had said he would not seek.

Van Buren returned on July 5, and as soon as he stepped off the boat, he must have realized his good fortune in having avoided American politics for a year. At exactly that moment, the Bank of the United States was trying to renew its charter and a new tariff was being coaxed through Congress. Both issues fell exactly on the fault line that was so troubling for the Jacksonians, between supporting the economy and avoiding intrusive government, and Jackson's cabinet was predictably divided. A letter from Jackson was waiting for Van Buren the moment he arrived in New York, and he went straight to Washington, where he found a spectral Jackson determined to prevail in yet another mortal struggle. With his usual penchant for direct observation, the president put the matter simply: "The bank, Mr. Van Buren, is trying to kill me, but I will kill it!" Three days later, Jackson issued his famous veto of the bank charter, denouncing policies that make "the rich richer and the potent more powerful." The Bank's director, Nicholas Biddle, howled, "It has all the fury of a chained panther, biting the bars of his cage."

And so ensued the next great political crisis for the Jacksonians, a crisis that ultimately ended with Jackson's veto of the bill to renew the bank charter but stoked more fires within the Democracy, increasingly torn between its Northern and Southern wings. Van Buren's political barometer was a little less reliable than usual during the bank crisis. As a New Yorker, Van Buren felt more sympathy with the central bank than did the clique of Westerners who surrounded Jackson and had gained influence during his tenure abroad—but in the long run, he was powerless to stop a policy that had grown into an obsession for Jackson. He was particularly slow to embrace the second phase of the plan—the removal of federal deposits—though ultimately he came aboard. He wrote Jackson, with all the enthusiasm of a recent convert, "The ground, that this is in truth a question between Aristocracy and Democracy, cannot be too often or too forcibly impressed upon the minds of the people."

The Jacksonians also had to deal with a resurgent Calhoun, now operating with all of the avenging fury of an angel cast out of heaven. His nullification doctrine had advanced beyond the Jefferson Day dinner, and in 1832 he and Jackson circled each other, each threatening to push the argument to its conclusion—in Calhoun's case, secession, and in Jackson's case, martial law. The president was on the verge of asking for volunteers to put down Calhoun's "treason" and crush "this wicked faction in its bud." He compared nullification to "a bag of sand with both ends opened," adding that "the moment the least pressure" was applied, the sand would flow out at each end. Again, Van Buren found himself uncomfortably in the middle, disliking Calhoun's stance but wanting to avoid an excess display of federal strength for many reasons. This time he was helpful, calming Jackson and working to bring down the tariff rates that Calhoun found so objectionable. The crisis passed without a great loss of face for either Jackson or Calhoun, but the lingering stench of nullification would remain in the air until 1860, when there was a lot more to nullify than a simple tax. The year 1832 was merely the dress rehearsal for a much larger production.

As difficult as the Bank and nullification crises were together, they offered one great advantage in their simultaneity. Van Buren and his allies could honestly claim to be occupying the vital center of public opinion in 1832, rejecting the extremes of both North and South to find a reasonable middle ground. In a sense, it was not so different from the role Van Buren had played throughout the 1820s, when he worked so hard to form the Democratic Party. But there were dangers all around—and as Jackson sounded more and more nationalistic during the nullification business, Northerners and Westerners extended feelers, wondering if the time was ripe for a "Union" party that would stop taking orders from the stagnant South. Van Buren did all he could to quell such initiatives—they were damaging to his chances and to his unwavering idea of a national party on Jeffersonian principles.

As these disuniting tendencies were gathering steam, Van Buren's idea of a two-party system received support from an unlikely source—a new party that sprang into existence for the express purpose of defeating Jackson and Van Buren. The Whigs, as they were ultimately known (for opposing Jackson as the revolutionary Whigs had opposed George III), were an unlikely batch of Northern quasi-Federalists and Southern states' rightists, allied more through alienation than shared principles. They had great luminaries, including Webster, Clay, and, for a while, Calhoun, now officially a nonperson in the Jacksonian universe, removed with all the surgical cleanliness of a Soviet apparatchik arranging dignitaries on the May Day reviewing stand.

The election of 1832 posed no difficulties for the Democratic slate, and Jackson easily outdistanced his principal challenger, Henry Clay. As vice president, Van Buren was a reliable helpmeet, generally sustaining Jackson in the policies he had embarked upon, occasionally reining him in, and rarely objecting outright, even when the president pursued policies that reflect poorly on his complex legacy (Cherokee removal, slavery). Without quite revolutionizing the office, it is safe to say that Van Buren sharpened it and gave it more relevance than it would have again for some time. Jackson and Van Buren were clearly part of a team in a way that Calhoun never was—and their triumphant tour of New York and New England in the summer of 1833 was a brilliant bit of grandstanding that did much to build the party. It must have been gratifying to preside over the Senate that had recently rejected him, and he performed his duties with his trademark combination of shrewdness and levity. One day in 1834, after a tirade by Henry Clay against Jackson's economic policy, allegedly ruinous to Clay's backers, Van Buren walked to Clay, then loudly asked him if he could borrow a pinch of "fine maccaboy snuff." Even his enemies laughed at this well-acted political theater.

The business of presidential succession usually gets serious about two years before the actual election. Van Buren was nothing if not punctual, and around 1834 the rumor mills began ginning up arguments and counterarguments over his suitability for the White House. It was a particularly difficult succession for a number of reasons. There were a number of hurt feelings to soothe—not only had Jackson trampled on delicate sensibilities North and South (and the Whigs censured him in 1834), but Van Buren had outmaneuvered a huge number of politicians who considered themselves his social betters and could not quite understand what he was doing on the pedestal. As we might expect, Calhoun was at the front of that list, and he denounced Van Buren with withering sarcasm on the floor of the Senate: "He is not of the race of the lion or the tiger; he belongs to a lower order—the fox."

There were many different insecurities that united the Van Buren haters. Some faulted him for being too generous to Catholics (he had written a sympathetic letter to the Vatican in 1829) and wondered if he was at the center of a "popish plot." Some were alienated that a party system existed at all and wished for a return to a mythical cloud-cuckoo land where all Americans worked together in harmony. Some loathed him for the perceived attack on the Bank—and others for not doing enough to destroy banking systems in general (a disturbing number of radical factions in the New York Democracy were spinning out of control). Many were angry that Van Buren seemed too Southern, and appeared to cosset slavery every chance he got. Many others were upset that he seemed too Northern, had opposed slavery's expansion at key moments, and was insufficiently attuned to Southern needs. The South was especially exasperating since he had spent the better part of a decade cultivating allies there. With uncharacteristic emotion, he poured out his feelings to a Southern friend (a woman, of course): "God knows I have suffered enough for my Southern partialities. Since I was a boy I have been stigmatized as the apologist of Southern institutions, & now forsooth you good people will have it . . . that I am an abolitionist." For a time he carried a pair of loaded pistols to work in the Senate.

What was revolutionary about Van Buren—that he was a professional politician—rubbed many people the wrong way as he stood on the penultimate step of his long political journey. It did not help, either, that Jackson had found so many enemies (and generally defeated them) during his second term. Whenever a strong president prepares to leave the scene, there is always a price to pay, and it was hardly surprising that Van Buren, who had aroused wrath throughout his career, would be expected to pay it. William H. Seward, the young Whig from Van Buren's backyard, called him "a crawling reptile, whose only claim was that he had inveigled the confidence of a credulous, blind, dotard old man." Nicholas Biddle, seething with rage after the Bank's defeat, predicted, "These banditti will be scourged back to their caverns."

Something about Van Buren's size and shape also appealed greatly to the rising number of humorists writing about politics, some of whom were merely funny, and others downright scabrous. It was both a curse and a blessing that a print revolution was rocking the political world—for sympathetic biographies were quickly disseminated, but more than a few hilarious burlesques of the Little Magician as well. Davy Crockett was especially brutal, calling him "Aunt Matty," "the perlitest cretur amongst the wimmen," imagining him "laced up in corsets," and suggesting that "it would be difficult to say, from his personal appearance, whether he was man or woman, but for his large *red* and *gray* whiskers." The writer Nathaniel Beverley Tucker, with support from Calhoun, published a thinly disguised novel, *The Partisan Leader*, in 1836, depicting Van Buren as "daintily dressed," wearing "delicate" slippers, and showing off hands that were "fair, delicate, small and richly jeweled." It would have been less damaging to call him a serial killer (as, in fact, people did call Jackson).

But Van Buren had one great weapon in his arsenal that no other candidate possessed: Andrew Jackson's blessing. Through party newspapers, through private meetings with his chieftains, and through any other means he could think of, Old Hickory sent the word out to the faithful that he wanted Martin Van Buren to be the next president of the United States. It had a tremendous impact. The infighting died down, and Van Buren easily won nomination at the Baltimore convention held in May 1835, far ahead of the election. The vice presidential candidate was Richard Mentor Johnson of Kentucky, a hero of the War of 1812.

Throughout the campaign, Van Buren conducted himself as candidates were expected to: by doing absolutely nothing. True to his nature, he gave rather bland indications of his middling position on the issues to the movers and shakers who needed confirmation that he would not stir the pot too much. The Whigs threw three different regional candidates at him (Daniel Webster, William Henry Harrison, and Hugh Lawson White), hoping that they could force the election into Congress, but Van Buren outpolled them, winning 170 electoral votes to their combined 124 and 762,978 popular votes to their 736,250.

At the age of fifty-three, Martin Van Buren was in the ascendant. He was the youngest president elected to date. At long last, the pilgrimage that had begun in Kinderhook had brought him to his life's destination. As a child, he had fallen asleep at night listening to political arguments in his father's tavern. Now, he had achieved what no one from New York ever had—what no one whose ancestors were not English ever had—and what no one from his gifted cohort of senators ever would. There are no records of his innermost thoughts in this moment of supreme triumph, but looking back at his extraordinary career—his childhood humiliations at the hands of the gentry, his genius for using party structures to defeat Clinton and Calhoun, his rejection for the England post, his stunning comeback—was it not obvious that an unseen hand was guiding his career forward? He could not be blamed too much if he expected the same sort of good fortune to accompany him into the Executive Mansion, where he would presumably rule for at least two terms, and perhaps more, given his youth and the limitless growth of the state whose strength he rode like a Saratoga jockey.

Far away from these reveries, a few financial analysts noted with concern some early tremors in an economy that was growing by leaps and bounds but was utterly unregulated. In his farewell speech, the most important since Washington's, Jackson had warned of unchecked speculation by "the money power." South and west of Washington, Texans were preparing to launch their independent republic, having successfully wrested the province away from Mexico, to the great interest of slave owners looking for room to expand. But these were mere wisps of clouds, hardly noticeable as Van Buren surveyed the blue skies stretching before him.

———

5

Panic

After years of scraping, Martin Van Buren finally stood atop the Matterhorn of American politics. Like a mountain goat, he had leapt upward from one craggy promontory to the next. Now, there was nowhere higher to go—and he may have experienced the mountain goat's momentary confusion of wondering where to go when he reached the summit. But all in all, it was a happy time, filled with the things he liked best—parties, gossip, and cabinet appointments. He aimed for stability, keeping many of Jackson's appointees and leaning South with new choices. Balance always.

The year 1837 opened with the future looking very bright indeed. Van Buren was poised to become one of the great presidents. Everything in his career had tended to this moment. Surely he must have reflected that winter on his remarkable journey from an overcrowded tavern in Kinderhook to the White House. What a pleasure it must have been to remember all of the enemies who had tried to impede his progress; the social betters who sought to keep him down; the political rivals who underestimated him; the endless insults hurled his way. Now he would helm both the Democracy and the great republic itself. At last, a New York president! What a pity that Aaron Burr had died in September 1836—he would have enjoyed Van Buren's triumph. One can imagine that Van Buren envisioned a long and prosperous reign, followed by the chance to handpick a successor. He would be lionized forever and, centuries later, if an elegant series of presidential biographies was ever contemplated, historians would surely clamor to write his extraordinary life story.

All presidents-elect, presumably, have felt similar thoughts during their transition. But like the mortals they preside over, they, too, are controlled by the fates. All expect, on reaching the pinnacle, to succeed—but none finds unambiguous success. All expect to shape events, but find themselves shaped by them. All discover that no individual or government is entirely impervious to the external shocks that rain down on us from the heavens. That is why, for all our secularism, insurance policies still refer to "acts of God" as eventualities that cannot be prevented, no matter how much weatherproofing we build into our homes. Sometimes a disaster can elevate a president to immortality—the Second World War, for example, or the secession of the South. But most of the time, disasters are just depressing. The depression that struck the Van Buren presidency more than qualified. The Panic of 1837 was simply the worst financial catastrophe in American history until the Crash of 1929.

On March 4, there was no sense of what was looming, and so Van Buren's inaugural came off without a hitch. A "balmy vernal sun" shone on the proceedings, and a huge crowd of twenty thousand arrived for the coronation ritual. A local newspaper wrote, "Perhaps the city was never on any previous occasion so full of strangers." Jackson and Van Buren arrived at the Capitol in a coach made from the timbers of the USS *Constitution*, escorted by cavalry, infantry, and a band blaring patriotic music. Jackson still held sway; a popular writer of the day, N. P. Willis, recorded that "a murmur of feeling rose up from the moving mass below, and the infirm old man . . . bowed to the people." At the end of the ceremony, the crowd wildly saluted Old Hickory, and Thomas Hart Benton wrote, "The rising sun was eclipsed by the setting sun." Upon leaving town,

Jackson was said to have remarked that his only regrets were that he did not shoot Clay or hang Calhoun.

Van Buren acquitted himself gracefully. He spoke clearly, and his inaugural address, while not exactly scintillating, stands out from the tedium of nineteenth-century presidential rhetoric. He called attention to the anomaly of his relative youth and announced that a new generation was ready to lead America—a theme that would be used on many other occasions, particularly by Presidents Kennedy and Clinton. He used the fiftieth anniversary of the Constitution to give an unusually sweeping history of "the great experiment," arguing that the people had never let themselves down, and that the democratic idea would flourish so long as they retained the spirit of compromise. Toward that end, he spoke daringly about slavery, the first time the word had been mentioned in an inaugural (though Van Buren promised not to interfere with it). He ended the address with warm personal remarks for Jackson, wishing "a brilliant evening" to his "well-spent life."

For all of Van Buren's loyalty to Jackson, there was a sense of a new beginning—and nothing symbolized the new age more vividly than the snorting railroad that whisked Old Hickory back toward Tennessee—as close to Tennessee as the tracks ran (not very). Everywhere, change was in the air. The New York merchant Philip Hone wrote in his diary, "Hurrah for Martin the First!" In England, Victoria also assumed the throne in 1837—her reign would outlast Van Buren's by six decades.

Amid all the pomp and circumstance, there were ominous signs that all was not right with the republic, but few paid heed. A careful listener might have heard rumblings in the economy—hints of digestive distress that foretold far greater ills to come. In February, mobs in New York destroyed stores and warehouses to protest the high price of flour. Rising class tensions were equally visible in the way wealthy people described these protests. George Templeton Strong saw a New York demonstration and described it as "a convention of loafers from all quarters of the world."

Soon these rumblings turned into a roar. The diaries from that spring reveal a quick change from mundane entries about quotidian events to the chaos of an economic free fall. The word *panic* accurately conveys the emotional intensity of an event that was unprecedented in American history for its suddenness and severity. Van Buren may have had the briefest presidential honeymoon in history.

The first temblors were felt a mere thirteen days after he assumed office. On March 17, Hone wrote, "The great crisis is near at hand, if it has not already arrived." Over the next month, prices rose and financial houses fell like stacks of cards. In early May, the crisis peaked with the closing of major banks in New York. Hone wondered on May 8, "Where will it all end?—In ruin, revolution, perhaps civil war." On May 10, "The volcano has burst and overwhelmed New York." May 11: "All is still as death." May 12: "The commercial distress and financial embarrassment pervade the whole nation. Posterity may get out of it, but the sun of the present generation will never again shine out. Things will grow better gradually, from the curtailment of business, but the glory has departed. Jackson, Van Buren and Benton form a triumvirate more fatal to the prosperity of America than Caesar, Pompey and Crassus were to the liberties of Rome." Even more terrified, George Templeton Strong wrote, "God only knows what the consequences will be. Ruin here, and on the other side of the Atlantic, and not only private ruin but political convulsion and revolution, I think, would follow such an event. . . . Where in the name of wonder is this all to end?"

The Panic spread with a remarkable contagion (it was likened to the cholera epidemic that had just attacked New York) and soon overwhelmed Philadelphia, Baltimore, New Orleans, and every other commercial city. Its effects would ultimately spread around the world—to the great financial institutions of Europe, heavily invested in the explosive American economy, and to little communities in the remotest hinterland of Africa, where tiny U.S. missionary establishments were forced to shutter themselves for lack of funding. The British minister wrote that there was so much "terror" that Van Buren would soon be overthrown. One observer expected to see tumbrels and guillotines soon.* Finally, on May 15, the president called a special session of Congress to deal with the crisis.

What exactly had caused the Panic? That question continues to challenge historians. Economic history often takes a backseat to the more interesting stories of clashing personalities, and that may be especially true in the Jacksonian period, when the personalities were unusually lively and the money issues conspicuously less so. But of course financial decisions matter a great deal to the people who are affected by them at the time. Emerson conveyed some of the desperation of those weeks in a journal entry: "Cold April; hard times; men breaking who ought not to break; banks bullied into the bolstering of desperate speculators; all the newspapers a chorus of owls."

Van Buren's rise to power had coincided with an orgy of growth and speculation, beginning on Wall Street but fanning out to the four corners of North America and hardly stopping there. A huge amount of wealth was accumulated through traditional means—John Jacob Astor's fur empire in the West, and real estate tycoons grabbing up land wherever they could find it. But there was also a rage for novelty—new inventions, new clothing styles, new toys for the leisure time that Americans were discovering for the first time. Technological advances in printing allowed newspapers to flourish as never before, intensifying America's zeal for political gossip, fashion, and whatever bits of knowledge might be turned to competitive advantage in the brawling marketplace. The great Charles River Bridge case, argued before the Supreme Court throughout the 1830s, was resolved in 1837, liberating the corporation from its

---

*Another effect of the Panic is that it allowed Cornelius V. S. Roosevelt to assemble great wealth through the purchase of newly cheap lots in Manhattan. This boon would help launch the career of his grandson Theodore half a century later.

earlier constricting definition and dealing another Jacksonian blow to special privilege.

Perhaps nothing symbolized this unprecedented churning economy better than the railroad itself, the Internet of its day—fantastically high-tech, symbolizing speed, connectedness, and information. Tracks were laid as fast and as far as it was humanly possible to do, and for every railroad successfully built in the 1830s, there were a dozen more planned. It is difficult, in a short space, to encapsulate all that the railroad conjured in Van Buren's time, but the great range of emotions expressed on the subject, from astonishment to alienation, accurately conveys the size of the imaginative leap taking place. Emerson called the train whistle the voice of the nineteenth century. Hawthorne, whose first book came out in 1837, captured its excitement and dissonance:

> But hark! There is the whistle of the locomotive—the long shriek, harsh, above all other harshness, for the space of a mile cannot mollify it into harmony. It tells a story of busy men, citizens, from the hot street, who have come to spend a day in a country village, men of business; in short of all unquietness; and no wonder that it gives such a startling shriek, since it brings the noisy world into the midst of our slumberous peace.

To put it bluntly, people who had followed certain kinds of agrarian folkways for a millennium, in America and the Europe of their ancestors, were now feeling, for the first time, the mighty effects of unrestrained capitalism. Iron, steel, cloth, leather, and shipbuilding were especially strong—and all were located in the surging North. In 1835, New York City was by far the first commercial city in the United States—and it is a little astonishing to know that it was second in the world after London.

Like all great shifts, this had good and bad effects. Americans reveled in their new wealth, and much of it trickled down to ordinary families, but there was also a disturbing sense that something precious in the simple republican past was being thrown away, or worse, sold. As more and more goods moved from warehouses to stores to parlors around the nation, Americans could be counted on to devise tacky slogans to sell them. In the 1830s, Independence Hall in Philadelphia became a clothing store, with a sign that read, WE HOLD THESE TRUTHS TO BE SELF-EVIDENT, THAT ALL MEN ARE CREATED EQUAL—THAT THEY CAN OBTAIN CLOTHING AS RICH, AS CHEAP AND AS DURABLE AS AT ANY OTHER ESTABLISHMENT IN THE NATION.

Tocqueville noted our stunning acquisitiveness, and, like so much of what he wrote, his words ring true today. Leave it to a Frenchman to find the existential dread that still haunts a nation of Kmart shoppers:

A native of the United States clings to this world's goods as if he were certain never to die; and he is so hasty in grasping at all within his reach that one would suppose he was constantly afraid of not living long enough to enjoy them. He clutches everything, he holds nothing fast, but soon loosens his grip to pursue fresh gratifications. In the United States a man builds a house in which to spend his old age, and he sells it before the roof is on; he plants a garden and lets it just as the trees are coming into bearing; he brings a field into tillage and leave no other men to gather the crops; he embraces a profession and gives it up; he settles in a place, which he soon afterwards leaves to carry his changeable longings elsewhere. If his private affairs leave him any leisure, he instantly plunges into the vortex of politics; and if at the end of a year of unremitting labor he finds he has a few days' vacation, his eager curiosity whirls him over the vast extent of the United States, and he will travel fifteen hundred miles in a few days to shake off his unhappiness. Death at last overtakes him, but it is before he is weary of his bootless chase of that complete felicity which forever escapes him.

No one could exactly arrest this commercial zeal, but the climate of speculation raised hackles inside a Democratic Party that still clung to a Jeffersonian creed—a creed that was increasingly irrelevant to an economy that was obviously Hamiltonian, and then some. Many Democrats, especially from the West, complained about Wall Street and the invisible money changers who bought and sold their land before anyone had a chance to settle it. Western land sales rose from 1.9 million acres in 1830 to 12.5 million acres in 1837. To finance these sales, a huge number of shaky banks and shadowy middlemen came into existence (347 banks were chartered between 1830 and 1837 alone). As with the 1920s and 1990s, there was astonishment at how much wealth could be created through a few simple maneuvers on paper. Van Buren's lieutenant, Silas Wright, had a nightmare that the Bank had literally turned into a monster. Jackson's farewell address, the greatest between Washington's and Eisenhower's, pulled no punches as it attacked "the money power" in American life.

But the Democratic response was inconsistent. Predictably, Jackson agreed with the prevailing Western feeling that there was too much loose money in the economy and that speculators should be brought down a notch. Hence the infamous Specie Circular, a presidential directive in 1836 that forced all land to be purchased in hard currency, and Jackson's bitter war against Nicholas Biddle and the Bank of the United States (which may have restrained irresponsible speculation, despite Jackson's arguments). But many other Democrats felt uncomfortable with Jackson's simple hard-money remedies and worried about the constriction of credit that would follow. Unlike him, they felt that banks—especially state banks—were useful if they did their jobs properly, and they saw no need to impose eighteenth-century solutions on a booming nineteenth-century economy. To add to the confusion, the Democrats pursued a number of policies that fueled the very speculation they disliked, including the conversion of a federal deficit into a $28 million surplus, all of which was sent back directly to the states.

To sum up the situation, then, Van Buren inherited a superheated economy that was completely unregulated in some ways and draconically controlled in others. Even among his closest supporters, there was deep division over what the government should do to stimulate or suppress growth. The Whig opposition, on the other hand, felt cynicism toward anyone who claimed to be the heir of Jackson, and argued that the destruction of the Bank had eliminated what might have been a useful instrument of fiscal control (that point is still disputed by historians). There was too much loose credit and inflation in an economy that had become badly overextended through greed and speculation, and an unfavorable balance of trade with England deepened instability. All this added up to a tinderbox waiting for a match. The match was lit when a number of problems in England and Ireland forced a demand for payments from American bankers, who were unable to find the money to fulfill their obligations. To make matters worse, the price of cotton fell, and other crop failures further reduced the shrinking amount of credit available on Wall Street. Van Buren never knew what hit him.

Once confidence is lost, of course, it is nearly impossible to restore. The *Congressional Globe* recorded that "distrust seized upon the public mind like fire in the great prairies." Across the nation, a dark shroud now fell across what had seemed like a limitless future. With no credit available, no business could be started. Bankruptcies were recorded in huge numbers. Massive unemployment resulted (twenty thousand out of work in New York City), and almshouses had to turn away hundreds of deserving families. Ships listed idly in their berths. Breadwinners became beggars. Many died of starvation. Herman Melville's older brother Gansevoort lost his business, leaving the fatherless family penniless. Herman's decision to go to sea was a direct result of his poverty, so the cosmic rage of *Moby-Dick* is also traceable to the Panic of 1837.

This economic disaster soon became a political disaster as well. It took no time at all for the Whigs to blame President Van Buren, of course. He was guilty by association with Jackson, and he was also vulnerable to the charge that the government did little to relieve popular misery. A Whig paper pointed out "the melancholy truth, the awful truth, that the administration did nothing to relieve the distress." Things got so bad that Van Buren began drinking a potion of soot and water to calm his dyspepsia.

But there was only so much Van Buren could do. It was hard to know where to begin—like the cholera epidemic, the Panic seemed to have no beginning, middle, or end. Worse, he had no tools to work with, and, to some extent, that was his own doing. Since he had entered politics, Van Buren had called for less government and the dismantling of Hamilton's financial apparatus. In fact, he had personally supervised much of it. But now, with a sudden thud, he had reached the limits of Jeffersonian doctrine. What could he do to restore credit? How could he make money appear where there was none? What agency could he ask to feed the hungry and clothe the poor?

In this unenviable position, he did what most of us would have done—he arranged for a Panic session. Specifically, he called for Congress to meet in September to take special measures to alleviate the crisis. It was the first special session ever called that did not address a military crisis. All summer, he consulted with leading Democrats, which did not exactly solve matters, since they were badly divided. Some, like Jackson (still peppering Van Buren with angry letters about the Bank), wanted the government to maintain hard money and keep its distance from the financial world. Other influential leaders, especially in the crucial states of Virginia and New York, wanted him to ease credit with paper money and support state banks.

When Congress reassembled, Van Buren was ready. As usual, he had a little something for everybody. His message, delivered on September 5, was an impressive document, clear and concise. For the hard-money people, he offered to postpone the final distribution of the surplus and proposed that an independent Treasury be created for federal deposits—separate from the banks. This was a momentous step, one that had been discussed in the most anti-bank fringes of the Democracy, but never put into motion. For bankers, he offered to delay federal lawsuits against those that had suspended payments and urged that Treasury notes be created to get more money into circulation. All in all, it was an attractive proposal—perhaps a little short of what the *Washington Globe* called it ("the boldest and highest stand ever taken by a chief magistrate . . . the second declaration of independence"), but eminently practical.

Most of Van Buren's program sailed through Congress without significant opposition. But the most important proposal, the creation of an independent Treasury, caused consternation and brought out the underlying anxieties about money policy that had already released so much hot air into the House and Senate. Van Buren must have been gratified to see Calhoun come back into the fold and support his plan, but the speeches given by Calhoun and his fellow South Carolinians revived the specter of nullification and did more harm than good. After narrowly passing the Senate, the independent Treasury was defeated in the House.

Nor did Van Buren's problems end there. Bad luck always seems to attract more bad luck, and the Panic weakened him in two particular ways. It brought the Whigs exactly what they had been lacking—a unifying idea (that the Democrats had ruined the economy). And it chipped away at the adhesion that was so important to the Democratic cause. When Henry Clay came to a White House reception on New Year's Day, 1838, he complimented the president on having so many friends around him—to which Van Buren replied, sardonically, "The weather is very fine." The Panic exposed a fact that was not exactly Van Buren's fault, but which hurt him anyway—that try as he might, he was no Andrew Jackson when it came to inspiring people and uniting Americans from different backgrounds. Nearly every one of his steps brought criticism from one side or the other of the party he had founded (when you're on the left to begin with, there's always someone a little further to the left to make your life miserable).

Even in New York, he was hurting. A number of new political groups had sprung up in New York City in the 1830s, including the legendary Locofocos, a group of radicals who hated special privilege and supported hard money, the Bank war, and equal rights (their name came from a kind of match they used to illuminate a meeting one night when their opponents tried to keep them in darkness). Their ideas would flavor some of Van Buren's proposals, though he was never entirely one of them. At the same time, the Albany Regency upstate was worried about the anti-bank tenor of Van Buren's proposals. Even Van Buren's old friend Washington Irving felt "a strong distaste for some of those loco-foco luminaries who have of late been urging strong and sweeping measures." Unsurprisingly, the Panic weighed heavily on voters in the fall of 1837, and they sent the divided Democracy a dour message by voting heavily for the rising Whigs. The victors taunted Van Buren on election night by shooting off cannons near the White House. The Democrats would claw back over Van Buren's tenure, but the Panic had balanced the scales. A revealing encounter between presidents occurred in September 1837, when John Quincy Adams visited the White House to see how his old adversary and occasional friend was doing. Adams was impressed by his "composure and tranquility," but recorded Van Buren's heartfelt description of the "cares and afflictions" of the presidency and his wonder at "how universal the delusion was that anyone could be happy in it." One suspects that he was telling the truth.

No depression lasts forever, of course, and over his tenure as president, Van Buren would see the economic picture improve in a number of ways. By the spring of 1839, prices had almost regained their 1837 levels. But a second, smaller depression in the fall of 1839 sent the markets tumbling again and underscored how powerless Van Buren was to fix a financial system that had broken, with no repair manual inside Jackson's desk. The Independent Treasury bill finally passed in 1840, but it did not represent the great breakthrough that Van Buren had hoped for—and on which he had spent too much political capital. For all of Van Buren's political skill, his wizardry did not extend to Wall Street. It was not until his ideological descendant, Franklin Roosevelt, entered the White House that a modern system of regulation would bring the same economic balance that the founders had created in the political realm when they delicately calibrated every check and balance in the Constitution.

Every cloud has a silver lining, and a few aspects of the great Panic of 1837 are worth mentioning for historical interest, even if they did not exactly alleviate the nation's suffering or reverse Van Buren's plummeting fortunes. Sometimes a crisis can crystallize a feeling that is already in the air, and the Panic emphasized to Americans that, like Rip Van Winkle, they no longer lived in the familiar nation they had grown up with. In place of the sleepy agricultural republic that Jefferson had invented stood an economic colossus whose coughs and throat clearings sent shudders through counting-houses around the world. Van Buren had reorganized politics, but almost every other category of life was changing as quickly.

Another bright spot was how well Van Buren handled the press. In this regard, he was truly visionary. As he was preparing to inherit the presidency, Van Buren steered some money to a young Irish-American journalist, John Louis O'Sullivan, seeking to start an ambitious new magazine. The *United States Magazine and Democratic Review* became the liveliest monthly of its day, mixing Democratic political commentary with the freshest cultural writing available in the United States (Hawthorne published his stories there, as did a very young Walter Whitman, not yet Walt). Throughout the Van Buren era, if it can be called such, the *Democratic Review* took the lead in defending the new president, and defending him well. In issue after issue, O'Sullivan offered an eloquent defense of Van Buren and the Democracy, and did what partisan journals do best: shifted blame for the Panic to the other side (in this case, the late Bank of the United States).

Finally, the Panic is important because it empowered a kind of person who had never had much influence in American politics before. New York's Locofocos and other radical Democrats suffered the most from the Panic and then gave Van Buren some of his most creative ideas, including the independent Treasury and a few modest initiatives to improve working conditions. This may not have added up to much, but it was a beginning, and showed that for the first time a president was thinking about the urban poor. In the twentieth century, the great historian Frederick Jackson Turner would claim that the origins of progressivism lay in the Van Buren administration.

But for all these footnotes, it is clear that Van Buren's presidency was badly damaged by the Panic. Vulnerable to begin with, thanks to all the enemies he had made in his climb up the mountain, he now had a target on his back. Unlike the hair shirts that other presidents were forced to wear—Teapot Dome, Watergate—Van Buren had little to do with his disaster, but it was attached to him all the same. Such is the fate of presidents, and deservedly so—they get the glory and the blame. Had he encountered no other problems, Van Buren might well have recovered. Unfortunately, the Panic was only the first of many disappointments in store for the overeager republic.

Only ten years before Van Buren's election, Thomas Jefferson and John Adams had died on the same day, July 4, 1826, the fiftieth anniversary of the Declaration. Sermons across the land proclaimed that a special providence was guiding America's destiny, and it was hard at the time to refute the evidence. But now retribution was at hand. The Panic caused a terrible shock, both financially and, worse, psychologically. It drained confidence—that precious resource that Americans seem to drink in like oxygen. And the Panic was really only the surface manifestation of a huge number of other problems that suddenly were revealed in the harsher light that accompanies hard times. What had felt like effortless progress was badly interrupted in 1837. Everything Van Buren had worked to build—his party, his presidency, his reputation for political sagacity—was imperiled by the tsunami that struck at almost the exact moment he took office.

6

Shadows

At first, the severe shock of the Panic obliterated the other issues on the presidential docket. Most presidents would have considered that plenty to work through. But even as the financial picture began to brighten, it became clear that there was no shortage of adversity facing President Van Buren and that many problems required the most delicate executive attention. Van Buren was used to hard challenges and prided himself on his reputation as a gifted fixer of crises that others could not solve or even foresee. But now that he was president, the problems seemed to multiply, as if the Panic were a Pandora's box, forcing other types of anxiety out into the open. Financial vulnerability will do that to a nation or, for that matter, to a family—magnifying even the tiniest defect before the minute self-examination that accompanies economic failure.

Suddenly, and for what felt like the first time in American history, Americans began to look with new skepticism at the national narrative, seeing a more complex portrait than Parson Weems's bromides about George Washington. The United States was no longer a simple agricultural republic in 1837—it was a society of clashing economic interests, people moving in all directions, savage Indian removals, boatloads of immigrants, growing pockets of despair, and politicians who could barely speak to one another.

The New Deal photography of the 1930s contains an unusual amount of contrast—striking areas of blackness next to brilliant sun-drenched objects in the foreground—aptly mirroring the shifting moods of the Depression. In a similar way, the problems of the 1830s cast long shadows over America. There is a darkness to Poe and Hawthorne, both emerging at exactly this moment, that cannot simply be explained by their fascination with the supernatural.

One problem, of course, dominated all the others, and it too was brought uncomfortably into the sunlight by the Panic of 1837. Slavery was anything but a tiny defect. It was the most glaringly undemocratic idea in our history, so powerful that we are still wrestling with its legacy in the twenty-first century. But until Van Buren's administration, it was largely invisible as a matter of public discourse. To be sure, it existed, and Americans knew of it. But it was not generally an issue in political campaigns or newspaper headlines or speeches on the floor of Congress. After the founders failed to resolve the slavery question, predicting that it would disappear naturally over time, it hardened into an impasse, with the South generally prevailing in its desire not to discuss the matter. All that was about to change.

To visit the United States in the 1830s, as many foreign travelers did, was to see two Americas. North of the Mason-Dixon Line, visitors could marvel at all the signs of an aggressively entrepreneurial culture, wheezing and humming in the open air of the bustling nineteenth century. There were railroads, newspapers, cheap books, factories, and a culture of connectedness not too different from what the world feels now in the so-called age of globalization. Business depended on information and speed; all three depended on the railroad—the literal engine of capitalism.

But if that same traveler peered across the invisible boundary separating North and South, he would see a very different world. Instead of machinery, human beings generated the power needed for the local economy to function. Instead of increasing openness and information, a small population of privileged landowners controlled all access to news and political power. Instead of democracy, feudalism prevailed—a feudalism based on race hatred. Visitors noticed, and Americans, always sensitive to foreign opinion, began to ask themselves what kind of country they aspired to be. And so, for this and other reasons, slavery came out from the shadows and into the daylight of American politics.

The consensus not to regulate or even discuss slavery began to erode during Van Buren's presidency, with profoundly destabilizing results that would ultimately smash the political edifice he had built. If the Panic had destroyed confidence in the economy, the slavery debates undermined the certainty that the Union was perfect and perpetual, as Jackson and Van Buren had said that memorable night in their toasts to Calhoun. Jackson, whose strong sympathy for slavery was well known, had kept the lid clamped tight on abolition. But the election of Van Buren threw a new spotlight on the growing slavery debate, in part because he was a Northern president, and in part because his own views on the subject were difficult to decipher—leading advocates on both sides to project their own feelings onto him, assuming he was on their side or, just as often, that he was in league with their opponents.

In truth, it is difficult to pin down exactly where Van Buren stood on the topic. The answer depends very much on the year and the context in which he was forced to express his feelings. Throughout his career, he had a remarkable ability to absent himself from a contentious slavery vote just before it was called, and his private papers are surprisingly free of any reference to the issue—but perhaps that is not so surprising. Most Americans barely think of him in the context of slavery at all, or dismiss him as a spineless courtier of the South—the dastard portrayed in the 1997 film *Amistad*. But that is too shallow a first impression. It is truer to see the entire struggle taking place in microcosm inside him.

There is certainly plenty of evidence to suggest that he favored slavery or, to be more precise, that he saw no reason to derail his political career with intemperate objections to it. From the beginning of his public life, going back to the War of 1812, he had pursued an ingenious Southern strategy, cultivating friends below the Mason-Dixon Line who could help him advance and whose enemies in New York were generally the same as his own. This was not merely a selfish decision, though it certainly facilitated his advancement. It was the accurate assessment of a master vote-counter, who understood instinctively that the South had to join him if he was going to succeed in building a new national party. Robert Caro's brilliant study of Lyndon Johnson's ambitious climb through the Senate portrays an equally sharp student of politics making the exact same calculus over a century later.

It is impossible to re-create the seminal conversation that took place between Van Buren and Jefferson in 1824, in the course of Van Buren's pilgrimage to Monticello, but we can assume that slavery came up, since it was Jefferson's obsession during the last decade of his life. Whenever Van Buren felt the need to shore up his credentials or to strengthen the reach of the party he was building, he took another extended trip through the Southern states. His reward was relatively little opposition to his selection as vice president and then president.

Needless to say, Van Buren was disinclined to disturb these friends if he could avoid it. If his inaugural was the first to mention slavery—a modest step forward—it did so by promising that he would never tamper with it. Like most of his predecessors, he was a former slave owner himself (he had owned a slave named Tom, who ran away), a credential that separated him in an important way from the two other Northerners, both Adamses, who had held the presidential chair. His ties to the South became significantly more personal in November 1838, when his eldest son, Abraham, married Angelica Singleton, the daughter of a wealthy planter from South Carolina and the cousin of Dolley Madison. For the rest of his presidency, she would act as his hostess, cloaking all White House events with the magnolia scent of Southern hospitality.

There is no doubt, whatever his private sympathies, that he did all he could to suppress the early spread of anti-slavery materials. As New York abolitionists began to take concerted action in 1835, on the eve of his presidential bid, he ordered his cronies to take measures against them, disrupting their meetings and preventing them from sending anti-slavery material through the mails. As petitions continued to flood Congress, Van Buren joined with the South in refusing to listen to them. The so-called Gag Rule proposed by Henry Pinckney of South Carolina ordered that all abolitionist tracts be tabled before they could be read—an outrageous violation of free speech. It passed the House in May 1836, exactly as Van Buren was launching his run, and he happily supported it. No abolitionists would stop him from getting to where he needed to go.

That is the bulk of the evidence against Van Buren. But there is also some evidence to suggest that his personal feelings tended in the opposite direction. Despite all he did to shore up his Southern credentials, there was always a lurking fear among Southerners that Van Buren was secretly anti-slavery. Opponents pored over his voting record, looking with special fascination at his actions in the New York Constitutional Convention of 1821. During those debates, Van Buren had been characteristically moderate, advocating that African-Americans should vote if they possessed a certain amount of property (a requirement that disenfranchised most), but the South never lost its paranoia that Van Buren had advocated voting for blacks. In 1834, he was accused in Mississippi of seeking to emancipate the slaves by act of Congress, and rumors persisted that he was a closet abolitionist. Even Abraham Lincoln would play on these fears in an early debate against Stephen Douglas around 1840, arguing that Van Buren had gone too far to empower black Americans!

In fact, what had worked so well for Van Buren was not that he ardently supported slavery, or that he fought it, but that he was perceived as a reasonable thinker who could bridge opposing points of view. No one elected from New York could have survived if he was perceived as the agent of another region's interests. And no one knew New York better than Van Buren. But these middling sentiments began to work against him as the two sides of the slavery debate pulled apart, leaving the center difficult to hold. Van Buren's timing had been exquisite during his rise to the presidency, but now fortune turned against him for a second time. First, the Panic had struck a death blow at his presidency. Now the slavery debate was turning acrimonious, making normal politics impossible.

Why did the long conspiracy of silence, dating back to 1787, fall apart exactly as Van Buren inherited the presidency? To some extent, it was simply the right time. Sixty years had elapsed since the soaring claims of the Declaration of Independence had resonated around the world. In 1833, England had jolted the United States by freeing her slaves across the empire (an act that was completed in 1838). Even Mexico, behind the United States in so many ways, abolished slavery in 1829. Sometimes a mood changes quickly, as when *Sputnik* orbited above North America for the first time, or the Tet Offensive changed the tenor of the Vietnam War. Slavery simply grew more obvious and more odious in the late 1830s. Many Americans, aware that it was hypocritical to talk of slavery and freedom in the same breath, were no longer willing to avert their eyes and look in another direction.

Part of the answer also lies in the word *inherited*. The struggle for Jackson's succession had been unusually bitter and, like jealous siblings, Van Buren's many enemies were not exactly eager to help him launch a new phase of Northern domination. The same demographic changes that thrilled foreign observers terrified Southerners, who were determined to resist the North's growing political power. Two weeks before Van Buren's inaugural, on February 18, 1837, Calhoun wrote, "I had no conception that the lower class had made such great progress to equality and independence. Such change of condition and mode of thinking on their part indicated great approaching change in the political & social condition of the country, the termination of which is difficult to be seen. Modern society seems to be rushing to some new and untried condition."

But there is more to it than broad historical trends. For several specific reasons, the South was alarmed about slavery in the 1830s. The decade had started inauspiciously with the savage Virginia revolt led by Nat Turner in 1831, whose killing spree had left fifty-five whites dead and had traumatized the entire region. It had gone from bad to worse as abolitionists began to organize in the North and to disseminate publications to a broad audience of indignant Americans. In a sense, this was a double insult to the South, attacking the peculiar institution upon which the Southern economy was based and flaunting high-tech printing technology to do it.

The change did not happen overnight, and most Northern Democrats were still in the strange position of denouncing both slavery and abolition, believing that abolitionism was a form of fanaticism. But anti-slavery stock rose rapidly in the late 1830s, and each speech in Congress drove the wedge in deeper. Van Buren's election fell precisely on all of these fault lines—between regions, between parties, and between degrees of belief that a Slave Power was secretly governing the United States. In other words, exactly as he became president in 1837, the great North-South coalition that he had built came under a dark cloud. In November 1837, an abolitionist printer, Elisha P. Lovejoy, was brutally murdered at his press in Alton, Illinois, by a pro-slavery mob. John Quincy Adams said that Lovejoy's murder sent "a shock as of an earthquake throughout this continent."

Strong leadership was needed in this overheated climate, and Van Buren was in a tight spot. If he denounced slavery, half his party would walk out on him. If he did too much to coddle slavery, his home state would reject him. In 1837, there were 274 abolition societies in New York alone. He was left precariously trying to straddle two objects that were moving apart from each other. Neither was headed to the destination he wanted.

Still, it's important to point out that Van Buren showed some
moments of character during a generally dispiriting time. His kind-
ness toward one of his most vehement critics was a case in point.
William Leggett was one of the best journalists in New York, a
champion of the Democracy, workers' rights, the Bank war, and
many of Van Buren's specific reforms—but an outspoken opponent
of slavery and particularly the suppression of free speech relating to
slavery. Around Van Buren's election, he began to excoriate Van
Buren for his coddling of the South and, shortly after, became seriously ill. Leggett was amazed when Van Buren responded by
appointing him a diplomatic agent to Guatemala to improve his
health. The cure did not succeed, but the act restored the faith of
some of Van Buren's Northern critics.

But as this anecdote also reveals, Van Buren was losing some of
his best supporters and weakening the moral imperative that had
helped to create the Democracy in the first place, when it had a
claim on the affections of ordinary Americans who felt shut out of
the political process. As the slavery crisis deepened in the late
1830s, Van Buren was badly caught in the crossfire. To some extent
he was a prisoner of his own creation—for the heightened popular
interest in the political world, inflamed by party machinery and
political journals, now made it very difficult to flimflam one's way
out of a problem. The pleasant obfuscation that had made life bear-
able for politicians was no longer possible, owing to the strides in
printing and transportation that made every politician's speeches a
matter of public record. In other words, it was impossible to lie in
one location and then come home and deny that one had said such
a thing.

The central problem that now lay before him was brutally difficult: how to preserve the great Democratic coalition and move
beyond the slavery debate, while assuring followers that "democracy" actually meant something, and that dissenting views were
taken seriously; how to show people that America stood for

meaningful ideals while, there in broad daylight, slaves were sold as chattel within shouting distance of Congress.

In truth, there was something very wrong with Washington, D.C.—not just its slave markets but an ugliness that seemed to proceed from slavery and taint everything around it. Many travelers noticed it, and Americans winced at their descriptions. An English writer, James Silk Buckingham, lamented that here were found "persons of the least personal beauty, the plainest dresses, and the rudest personal manners that we had before remembered to have been congregated anywhere in America." He did not remember "a single instance in which any literary or scientific topic was the subject of conversation," and concluded, "There seemed, in short, united in the circles of Washington all the pretensions of a metropolis with all the frivolity of a watering-place, and the union was anything but agreeable." Buckingham also disliked the moral climate of a city that was not neutral at all on the great question of the day, but very actively pro-slavery. He noticed with horror the newspaper advertisements for both slave auctions and runaway slaves, and recorded with disdain that a local performance of *Othello* had resulted in a newspaper editorial calling for the lynching of the playwright—although Shakespeare would not have been easy to catch.

Some of the pressures ginning up the slavery debate were in fact extrinsic to the United States—though just barely. In 1836, Americans living in Texas—then a province of Mexico—declared an independent republic and almost immediately sought to join the Union. Andrew Jackson had championed the acquisition of Texas, but Van Buren was far less enthusiastic, knowing that the arrival of this much potential slave territory would inflame the North. After becoming president, he delayed full recognition for months, and then delayed Texan demands for annexation as well. Both sides were angry—John Quincy Adams saw in Van Buren little more than Jackson's expansionism "covered with a new coat of varnish," while Southerners denounced Van Buren for his timidity. Jackson wrote edgy letters to his successor, demanding stronger action and crossing well beyond the bounds of postpresidential propriety.

Van Buren offered more satisfaction to the South as he pursued a different Jacksonian legacy. Throughout his presidency he continued the brutal Indian removals that had freed up vast quantities of land in Jackson's Southwest. Thousands of Cherokees were forced to march along the "Trail of Tears" from Georgia to Oklahoma, and the Seminoles in Florida were violently hunted down (their leader Osceola was tricked into capture with a false flag of truce). Van Buren dwelt in the lying pieties of the day when he reported to Congress that the government's treatment of the Indians had been "directed by the best feelings of humanity." One of his favorite nieces, an insubordinate teenager, told him she hoped he lost the election because of what he and Jackson had done to the natives.

But as he placated the South, Northerners began to feel that this hypocrisy and violence, in both Florida and Texas, was connected by an invisible thread to the great Slave Power that seemed to dictate policy from Washington. Thirty years later, as he reviewed the causes that had led to the Civil War, the Massachusetts theologian Theodore Parker wrote, "Slavery was using the Union as her catspaw—dragging the Republic into iniquitous wars and enormous expenditures, and grasping empire after empire thereby."

Renewed pressures to gag discussion of slavery in Congress were also causing strain. In the fall of 1837, as Van Buren was straining to repair the economy, Congress took up a long debate over slavery in the district. Calhoun, having relinquished his designs on the White House, had emerged as the chief defender of the Southern Way, and that December he presented six resolutions that defended the peculiar institution in stronger language than Congress had ever heard. Most Democrats in the Senate supported him, implying that the White House approved. In the House, former president John

Quincy Adams was equally active, denouncing slavery in speech after speech, and earning lasting fame in his final incarnation as "Old Man Eloquent." It was a sign of how volatile the debates in Congress were that a duel ensued between Representatives Jonathan Cilley of Maine and William Graves of Kentucky. Cilley was killed, and Washington was plunged into deep mourning. Nathaniel Hawthorne, a college friend of Cilley's, wrote a stinging eulogy in the *Democratic Review*, essentially accusing the Slave Power of killing him.

To appreciate the full import and the even fuller strangeness of the slavery debates roiling Congress, it is worth pausing for a moment to reflect on the man who was presiding over the Senate as the chief representative of the administration. Van Buren's vice president, Richard Mentor Johnson of Kentucky, had made his career as an Indian fighter—alleged to have killed Tecumseh—and was a loyal Democrat. Like Jackson and Van Buren, he had fought against debt imprisonment and was popular with Northern workers. He didn't care too much for ceremony, or comb his hair, and Harriet Martineau wrote, "If he should become President, he will be as strange-looking a potentate as ever ruled." But the most striking fact in his personal background, an open secret in Washington, was his unusual domestic arrangement: Johnson was living openly with and was probably married to one of his slaves.

Early in his life, Johnson had fallen in love with a woman named Julia Chinn, a mulatto whom he inherited from his father. By her he had two striking daughters, Imogene and Adaline, and he treated all three as his family members, seating them at dinner with guests and traveling publicly in a carriage together. Johnson paid for his daughters' tutoring "until their education was equal or superior to most of the females in the country," and his wife ran his estate during his long absences on government business. But for all these progressive ideals, Johnson's attempt to integrate his family with local society failed, and a local newspaper article reported hauntingly that "they never circulated among the whites."

Julia died of cholera in 1833, but Johnson found a new consort, described in a remarkable letter from Amos Kendall to President Van Buren in 1839, recounting a visit to Johnson's "watering establishment" in Kentucky. Kendall was amazed not only by the vice president's happiness "in the inglorious pursuit of tavern keeping," but that he was spending time in the presence of "a young Delilah of about the complection of Shakespears swarthy Othello," "said to be his third wife . . . some eighteen or nineteen years of age and quite handsome." If anything had happened to Van Buren during his presidency, this young African-American woman would have become the first lady of the United States—if the nation could have withstood the shock, which of course it could not have.

The truly remarkable aspect of this story, obviously, is not that it happened but that Johnson was so honest about it. That masters were forcing themselves on their slaves was hardly a secret—the South Carolina novelist William Gilmore Simms, a prominent defender of slavery, wrote in 1838 that one of slavery's great benefits was that it allowed men to "harmlessly" vent their lust on their slaves. But because Johnson chose love over lust, the South despised him. His great crime was that he refused to be a hypocrite, and for that he paid a severe price.* Van Buren's Southern supporters, including Jackson, tried to remove Johnson from the ticket in 1840, but Van Buren resisted, adding to the strain that was developing between the old friends as the slavery debate deepened and they felt themselves instinctively to be on opposite sides of the divide. When Johnson finally died in 1850, his brothers forced a local court to issue a document proclaiming that he had never had children.

---

*A typically malicious song:

> The wave that heaves by Congo's shore,
> Heaves not so high nor darkly wide
> As Sukey in her midnight snore,
> Close by Tecumseh Johnson's side.

.   .   .

There were hundreds and thousands of other incidents that deepened America's racial worries during Van Buren's four years in
office, most of which have vanished from the history books, but
which show plainly a nation on a course to conflict. Frederick
Douglass escaped from slavery in 1838, making his way from
Maryland to Massachusetts, where he launched one of the most
remarkable careers of the nineteenth century. In 1840, a naval
court-martial case in North Carolina resulted in the conviction of
an officer who had flogged his sailors, but it hit a snag because some
of the witnesses were black and their testimony was illegal in that
state. When Van Buren upheld their right to testify in a naval case,
the South was furious.

Much better, from the Slave Power's perspective, and much
worse from our own, was Van Buren's performance during the celebrated *Amistad* case. In 1839, slaves had revolted and taken control
of the schooner *Amistad* off Cuba. Attempting to return to Africa,
they had instead landed at Long Island, and they were soon impris-
oned in Connecticut. Van Buren issued an executive order demanding that the slaves be taken to a naval vessel, to hasten their return
to their Spanish owners, but the case ground its way slowly through
the courts. Finally, in the last days of the Van Buren administration,
in February 1841, the seventy-three-year-old John Quincy Adams
delivered a stirring defense of the slaves before the Supreme Court,
winning their freedom and his glory. An abolitionist wrote that Van
Buren's executive order ought to be "engraved on his tomb, to rot
only with his memory."

About the worst thing that can happen to your reputation is to
be cast as the villain in a popular Steven Spielberg film. Undeniably,
Van Buren's actions in the *Amistad* case deserve censure. But it is
difficult to imagine any president between John Quincy Adams and
Abraham Lincoln acting differently, and it helps to understand that
Van Buren was fighting several difficult battles at the same time.
Without Southern support in 1840, Van Buren had no chance to

pass his economic program, recover from the Panic of 1837, or win reelection. As I hope I have made clear, he was not consistently pro-slavery and often enraged the South with his tacit support for certain African-American rights. In 1848, he would go quite a bit further.

Still, it was obviously too little too late, or perhaps it was all just too soon. Decades later, one of Van Buren's biographers, the son of his old law partner, reminisced about the extraordinary crowd of Van Buren loyalists, mostly upstate New Yorkers, who had first seized control of the state and then the federal government for a few exciting years, before the South had reasserted control. In particular, he remembered a searing incident from that time, the heartbreaking story of an African-American government employee whose wife, a slave, killed their children after they were taken away and sold illegally. The author, William Allen Butler, then concluded with an interesting statement: "This was surely enough to make us all Abolitionists at heart, and such, I think, we all became."

That statement should be taken with a grain of salt, but still it offers a correction to the kneejerk way in which most people dismiss Van Buren as a stooge of the South. In the long run, neither his pro-slavery nor his anti-slavery actions were enough to forestall the defenestration that just about everyone in the United States knew was coming. Van Buren approached the intensifying debate over slavery the way that most politicians do—he danced around it, trying to placate people and offering various concessions to maintain his support. That philosophy works with the money and patronage issues that constitute the vast bulk of what passes for politics. But once in a great while, a cause will assume so much moral weight that it simply refuses to go away, and if a politician does not treat it with the seriousness it deserves, it destroys him. Lyndon Johnson discovered that in Indochina, and Van Buren's experience wrestling with slavery was not entirely dissimilar. The more he tried to hold the pieces of the Union together, the more they fell from his grasp. There was simply no center left for him to stand on, and without a center Van Buren was lost. By failing to take a stronger stand, the greatest politician of his generation had checkmated himself.

As he looked ahead to the 1840 election, there were already ominous signs. In New York, as Van Buren was acutely aware, anti-slavery Whigs were making great headway. Elsewhere, the two-party system was losing some of its sway, and abolitionists were launching a new Liberty party—a distant ancestor of the Republicans. Ultimately, it would take a new visionary to smash the system, as he had done, and build something better in its place. At the margins of the United States, a young political genius, even poorer than Van Buren had been, was giving his first speeches, exhorting the citizens of Illinois to build a government more truly worthy of themselves.

7

Chicanery

If Van Buren was beset by more than ordinary problems, he also drew on more than ordinary resources. His presidency may seem abbreviated and remote today, and to most Americans those four years in the 1830s might as well be pre-Columbian for all of their relevance to the bustling United States of the twenty-first century. After all, people were shorter then, and they built quaint structures whose inscriptions we do not always understand.

Still, the presidency is the presidency. Each of those years was as long, and felt as current, as any we have lived through before or since. Van Buren may have experienced more than his share of difficulty, but it would be a mistake to assume that he did not relish the role that he had prepared for since he was a young man.

His arrival in the White House in 1837 had signaled an exciting shift in the winds of Washington. While there was no doubt that he was Jackson's political heir, it was equally obvious that he was a very different person, and that social life in the capital would adjust accordingly. To begin with, he was much younger, a fact he trumpeted in his inaugural address: "I belong to a later age." There was something to the claim—Van Buren was the first president who was technically American, and not the bastard offspring of the British Empire. After his ascendancy, the nineteenth century was far more palpably in the air than during Jackson's tenure, with its royal mood swings and petty court disputes. The shift northward was also felt in the capital, and New Yorkers in particular were proud that one of their own occupied the executive mansion.

It would be an egregious exaggeration to call the Van Buren White House "Camelot," but the president's relative youth and affability quickened the pace of the capital. Four presidential sons entered the pool of eligible bachelors, and John Van Buren in particular showed an affinity for the role. "Prince John," as he was called after a celebrated dance with the young Queen Victoria, charmed men and women alike and was beginning to earn notice as a skilled politician in his own right. As mentioned earlier, Abraham Van Buren married a Southern belle, Angelica Singleton, to great acclaim in 1838. After returning from their honeymoon, they moved into the White House, where she took up the role of hostess with great zeal—perhaps too much zeal, for she enjoyed standing on a dais to receive her visitors, surrounded by female friends all dressed in white. Martin, Jr., was his father's principal secretary, and the two of them spent many nights together at dinner parties around Washington. Van Buren broke precedent by accepting invitations from cabinet members and prominent members of the opposition, restoring the broken link between the White House and Washington society. Even the dour John Quincy Adams was impressed, recording in his journal his guilty pleasure at staying too late at one party and returning with the two Van Burens in a carriage.

Large receptions were held at the White House as well—five thousand people came to his first formal open house in the spring of 1838. James Silk Buckingham described crashing a reception for three thousand, and coming away rather impressed by both the size and simplicity of American entertainments.

The president received his visitors standing, in the center of a small oval room, the entrance to which was directly from the hall on the ground floor. The introductions were made by the city marshal, who announced the names of the parties; and each, after shaking hands with the president, and exchanging a few words of courtesy, passed into the adjoining rooms to make way for others. The president, Mr. Van Buren, is about 60 years of age, is a little below the middle stature, and of very bland and courteous manners; he was dressed in a plain suit of black; the marshal was habited also in a plain suit; and there were neither guards without the gate or sentries within, nor a single servant or attendant in livery anywhere visible. . . . Everyone present acted as though he felt himself to be on a perfect footing of equality with every other person.

Not long after, the same writer recorded seeing Van Buren in church at St. John's:

The president walked into the church, unattended by a single servant, took his place in a pew in which others were sitting besides himself, and retired in the same manner as he came, without being noticed in any greater degree than any other member of the congregation, and walking home alone, until joined by one or two personal friends, like any other private gentleman. In taking exercise, he usually rides out on horseback, and is generally unattended, or, if accompanied by a servant, never by more than one. Everywhere that he passes he is treated with just the same notice as any other respectable inhabitant of the city would be, but no more.

But this informality did not mean he did not take his public responsibilities seriously. Van Buren upgraded the White House soon after his arrival, improving its plumbing and installing a crude version of central heating. To maintain his reputation as a generous host, he presided over lavish dinners as well. A Maine politician, John Fairfield, wrote a mouthwatering account to his wife, describing a meal that began with soup and continued with fish, turkey, beef, mutton, ham, pheasant, and a game bird that Fairfield could not pronounce (were there any edible animals left that he had not already mentioned?). Desserts included ice cream, jelly, almonds, raisins, apples, and oranges. These were not teetotaling events, either; liquid refreshment was plentiful, as it was throughout the early republic, in quantities that would stagger the more delicate political sensibilities of the twenty-first century.

The same generosity of spirit extended to the guest list. Van Buren was no stuffed shirt and enjoyed spending time with younger, creative people. Despite his lack of education, he was a far more versatile reader than Jackson, and from the outset his administration lent support to writers in the meager ways that it could. Many were encouraged to publish in the administration's literary organ, the *Democratic Review*, ably edited by John Louis O'Sullivan. An impressive number received jobs in the Van Buren administration, from the historian George Bancroft (who in turn hired Hawthorne and Orestes Brownson) to Washington Irving's friend James K. Paulding. Henry Longfellow was a Whig, and therefore could not support Van Buren, but he, too, felt welcome in the White House, and described an amusing visit in which Van Buren refused to divulge any political information: "We talked about the weather, the comparative expense of wood and coal as fuel, and the probability that as the season advanced it would grow milder!"

For all the problems occasioned by the Panic and the growing rift over slavery, these were exciting times for young intellectuals. After Emerson's call for a native body of expression independent from "the courtly muses of Europe," new writers answered the call, encouraged by the rapid pace of innovation in printing and the efflorescence of new newspapers and magazines. The popular hunger for political news that Van Buren helped to create—the sense that Whig-Democrat battles were a kind of spectator sport— helped writers and reporters eager to get their names into print (and up-and-coming political managers like Horace Greeley, who used the press to acquire influence).

In every domain of the intellect, a restless curiosity seized Americans, eager to build new frontiers wherever they could, and then to extend them again. The patent office groaned with the weight of new applications from a nation of tinkerers. Steamboats began to cross the Atlantic in April 1838, shrinking the distance between London and New York to a mere fortnight. The invention of the camera in France quickly led to the earliest American photographs, including, in 1840, the first ever taken of the moon (an early sign of America's proprietary interest). It is surprising that no one in France or England had thought to point a camera upward before, but Americans were always doing unusual things.

One of the more exciting examples of America's intellectual expansionism was a remarkable scientific expedition that set out in the summer of 1838 from Norfolk, Virginia, with six vessels and 346 men. The United States Exploring Expedition, or U.S. Ex. Ex., was the largest effort that had ever been mounted by the American government to advance human knowledge, and a worthy ancestor to the NASA missions of the 1960s. Its mission, no less daunting at the time, was the exploration of the little-known Southern Hemisphere and the remote reaches of the Pacific Ocean. The mission had received its original impetus from John Quincy Adams, but Van Buren took strong personal interest in it and gave much-needed encouragement to its leader, Lieutenant Charles Wilkes, when the navy seemed to take a dim view of the project. Despite considerable adversity, the U.S. Ex. Ex. would make history in a number of ways: the first oceangoing voyage of discovery by the U.S. government, the last all-sail naval squadron to circumnavigate the world, and a crucial extension of American force into Pacific regions that might as well have been extraterrestrial for their distance from the Yankee republic. All in all, before returning in

1842, the expedition logged 87,000 miles, mapped 800 miles of Oregon territory, and explored 1,500 miles of Antarctic coastline. Its Pacific charts were still being used a century later, in World War II.

Van Buren also encountered the world in other, less pleasant ways. Tensions with Great Britain had not entirely abated since his arrival on the political stage during the War of 1812, and during his presidency they flared up again along the long, poorly defined northern frontier. In the fall of 1837, a Canadian rebellion against Great Britain erupted just over the New York border, and drew support from many New Yorkers eager to renew the quarrel against their familiar enemy. In response to provocations, the British sent a militia to the American side of the Niagara River to board a vessel, the *Caroline*, which had been running supplies to the rebels. One American was killed, and rumors were soon circulating that exaggerated the attack. George Templeton Strong wrote in his diary, "It's infamous—forty unarmed American citizens butchered in cold blood, while sleeping, by a party of British assassins, and living and dead sent together over Niagara."

Van Buren was in a tight spot because what there was of the U.S. Army was already engaged putting down the Seminoles in Florida, but he asked the Northern state governors to help him cool tensions and to strictly enforce neutrality. While Van Buren protested the *Caroline* affair to the British ambassador, he was working behind the scenes to keep the conflict from growing larger. He was helped by his Regency friend Governor William Marcy, and by General Winfield Scott, who went to the border region and soon got things under control.

A year later, a very similar problem arose in a different location. The northeast border between Maine and Canada had never been settled properly, and the governor of Maine enraged the lieutenant governor of New Brunswick when he sent an expedition into the St. John River valley to clear out Canadian "trespassers." Soon militias were threatening one another on both sides of the border, and once again Van Buren sent Winfield Scott to calm things down. After some tense discussions in Washington, the American and British governments agreed to remove all troops from the area.

Both of these crises proved to be triumphs for Van Buren's cautious diplomacy, and the fact that he had been minister to the Court of Saint James certainly helped him to see the situation clearly. Similarly, Van Buren's decision to postpone the annexation of Texas was seen by many as a brave and prudent decision that flew in the face of his perceived allegiance to the Slave Power, but it cost him support from the volatile Southwesterners who were suspicious of Van Buren to begin with, including Andrew Jackson. All in all, Van Buren had an impressive foreign policy record during his tenure and showed more backbone than his accusers were inclined to admit.*

Van Buren also tried a few courageous measures on the home front. As the campaign year 1840 dawned, he realized that he had to do something to relieve conditions for the urban poor who were hit hardest by the Panic. It was too early in American history for any president—and especially a Jeffersonian—to offer direct relief. But on March 31, 1840, Van Buren issued an executive order creating a ten-hour day for federal workers, a dramatic step forward at a time when many employees worked from sunrise to sunset. Though Van

---

*Nor did his legacy end there. In 1841, a new secretary of state, Daniel Webster, reviewing the events of the *Caroline* affair, proposed an exacting definition of preemptive war to counter Britain's cavalier sense that it could arbitrarily invade the United States whenever it felt vaguely threatened. Webster insisted that a preemptive attack was only legitimate if the aggressor would prove "a necessity of self-defense, instant, overwhelming, leaving no choice of means, and no moment for deliberation." Amazingly, the Bush administration cited this as a rationale for its 2003 invasion of Iraq, though it would take a creative historian to argue that Iraq posed that kind of a danger, or, in fact, even as great a danger as disorganized American hotheads posed to Canada in 1837.

Buren did not take particular credit for the order at the time or later, it set an important precedent and showed skeptics that labor was more than animal strength, that people who worked deserved to be noticed, and that politics was about more than who could purchase influence. The Democratic platform that year had a plank that affirmed, in simple language, the Declaration of Independence, and thereby encouraged poor people from all races. The Slave Power would delete it in 1844, and it would not reappear until long after the Civil War.

But despite these breakthroughs, Van Buren had a serious image problem. To some extent, it was the same petty jealousy that had dogged his entire career. More than any president to date, he was criticized for the way he had maneuvered his way into the White House, and that distrust was exacerbated by the Panic of 1837 and the growing sectional rift. The more he tried to placate the North and South, the more he was perceived as an agent of one against the other. The more the economy foundered, the more easily everything wrong with modernity could be laid at his feet. If nothing else, he was an easily lampoonable president; his short stature and gigantic whiskers lent themselves well to cartooning, just emerging as an art form. Then there were a huge number of people who simply despised him for specific reasons he could not control: people who still loathed Andrew Jackson, people estranged from the government, people who hated any interference with the economy (Jabez Hammond wrote that "the whole banking interest was against him"). Those debits added up to a substantial negative balance.

Henry Adams called politics "the systematic organization of hatreds." But even from the distance of almost two centuries, it is difficult to fathom why the attacks on Van Buren were so relentless. He generally handled them well, impressing observers with his magnanimity, but one time he privately remarked, "Why the deuce is it that they have such an itch for abusing me? I tried to be harmless, and positively good natured, & a most decided friend of peace."

Sometimes the most amiable politicians arouse the bitterest enemies—Franklin Roosevelt, Ronald Reagan, and Bill Clinton immediately spring to mind. It's as if their enemies can't defeat them
through ordinary political tactics and have to resort to the narrow-
est shortcut: pure, unadulterated rage. Van Buren was accused of
every form of immorality. Because of the letter he had written to
the pope in 1829 assuring that Catholics were treated decently
in the United States, Whigs accused him of being secretly pro-
Catholic. Because he admired the South and had many friends
there, he was accused of being more pro-slavery than he was.
Because he came from the North, he was accused of abolition,
which also overstated his position. But perhaps the worst offense
that he was accused of, unforgivable in the aftermath of the Panic,
was personal extravagance.

It was not true, of course. But there was no denying that Van
Buren was careful about his appearance. Since that day when,
barely a teenager, he had been rebuked by his first employer, he had
never allowed himself to look like a country bumpkin. Now his fas-
tidiousness came back to haunt him, as his enemies at last found a
charge that would stick. A particularly grotesque speech against
Van Buren was given in Congress on April 14, 1840, just as the
presidential campaign was heating up, by a Whig representative
from Pennsylvania, Charles Ogle. Ogle was annoyed by an appro-
priations bill that had been sent by the White House to Congress,
asking for $3,665 to be paid "for alterations and repair of the Presi-
dent's House, and for the purchase of furniture, trees, shrubs, and
compost, and for superintendence of the President's grounds." He
also saw the chance for political blood sport. And so he gave a
wildly distorted, hilarious speech that attacked Van Buren for every
expenditure on the "Presidential Palace" that he had sought. The
speech was so thorough in its catalog of purchases that historians
still consult it, just to know what furniture was in the White House.

Ogle began by asking the people of the United States if they
were disposed to maintain a president in a "royal palace . . . as

splendid as that of the Caesars and as richly adorned as the proud-
est Asiatic mansion." He then went through all of the improvements that Van Buren had worked on, doubtless painstakingly, after
finally moving into the White House. There was the "President's
Garden," with its exotic plants, each of which sounded ridiculous
when Ogle intoned their names in both Latin and English—the vir-
gin's bower, the touch-me-not, and, perhaps worst of all, the false
foxglove.

Then Ogle moved on to the landscaping:

> No, sir; mere meadows are too common to gratify the refined
> taste of an exquisite with "sweet sandy whiskers." He must
> have undulations, "beautiful mounds, and other contrivances,"
> to ravish his exalted and ethereal soul. Hence, the reformers
> have constructed a number of clever sized hills, every pair of
> which, it is said, was designed to resemble and assume the
> form of AN AMAZON'S BOSOM, with a miniature knoll or
> hillock at its apex, to denote the n—ple.

Ogle sarcastically suggested the grounds would be improved by
a "colossal equestrian statue of Andrew Jackson with the little
Kinderhook magician mounted on beside him." Then he listed the
inventory of new furniture, selecting certain objects to fit his
theme . . . the French lamps with crystal globes, French mantel
timepieces, French comfortables, eagle-mounted French bedsteads,
and splendid French china vases. Inevitably, this kind of furniture
would lead to the ultimate in presidential decorating: "a royal
throne," with "a crown, diadem, scepter and royal jewels."

From there Ogle got downright mean. Continuing the French
theme, the cheapest insult in American politics, he lit into Van
Buren's character:

> It is worse, sir, because there is a degree of littleness in the
> thing which demonstrates as clearly as if it were written in

characters of living light, that the soul of Martin Van Buren is so very, very, very diminutive, that it might find abundant space within the barrel of a milliner's thimble to perform all the evolutions of the whirling pirouette avec chasse a suivant, according to the liberal gesticulation practiced by the most celebrated danseurs.

He finished with just about the worst thing that could be said about an American political leader:

How does the conduct of George Washington contrast on this subject with that of Martin Van Buren? Washington and Van Buren! Bless my soul, what a falling off! [Loud laughter.] Yes. What a fall was there, my countrymen! Then you, and I, and all of us fell down. After looking back down the long line of illustrious worthies who have occupied the Presidential chair in this country, is it not enough to make the heart of a patriot bleed, and to cover his cheek with blushes to see in what that illustrious line ends! What has Martin Van Buren ever done? Who can tell me? . . . I do not see what it is that such a nation as this should ever have made so much of so small a pattern of a man. He never originated any thing to benefit his country; he never fought to secure her glory; he has done nothing but plot to elevate himself; and yet here are we all thrown into turmoil about one little man, as if he was a hero or a statesman.

Needless to say, these charges were outrageous. Van Buren's crime was simply that he had upgraded a White House that was sorely in need of improvements. The Englishman James Silk Buckingham had gone to great lengths to describe the White House as "far from being elegant or costly" and "well adapted to the simplicity" of republican institutions, as was Van Buren's "plain suit of black." But there was an element of payback in Ogle's charges that made the barb more poisonous. As Ogle himself pointed out, the Jacksonians had made a great deal of hay out of John Quincy Adams's purchase of a billiard table and balls during the 1828 election—a charge that was as unfair as Ogle's. As the manager of that election, Van Buren was certainly accountable. His outmaneuvering of John Calhoun was also mentioned in the speech; Calhoun's partisans had never forgotten it. Now Van Buren received his comeuppance.

Politics is about endless moves and countermoves, but there was something ugly in the personal invective used against Van Buren that did not bode well for the future of democracy. Ogle's diatribe contained the seeds of countless future attacks against sitting presidents on the grounds of unseemly luxury—attacks that almost always came from people or parties who represented the party of privilege. Franklin Roosevelt and John F. Kennedy were dismissed as fraudulent by their critics merely because they had inherited wealth, as if it somehow tainted their politics. Bill Clinton was lambasted early in his first term for an expensive haircut. Al Gore was pilloried for the unavoidable fact that he had grown up in a Washington hotel while his father was a senator. In recent years, the Republicans scored points against John Kerry simply for looking French—the same word that Ogle used over and over to brilliant effect. His speech was the only thing that Charles Ogle ever did that passed into the history books, but it was significant, and damaging.

Yelping at the scent of a wounded fox, the Whigs threw everything into the campaign of 1840. It is still remembered as one of the great campaigns, and yet "great" seems too majestic a word for what was basically the cynical triumph of advertising over substance. After nominating the elderly military hero William Henry Harrison, the Whigs fell into paroxysms of excitement over the rumor that their candidate lived in a log cabin and had a fondness for hard cider. In fact, neither claim was true. Harrison was born into a considerably more substantial dwelling, an old brick mansion along the James River in Virginia. But that did not matter in the least. When in doubt, print the legend—and the image of an impoverished boy running around a log cabin entered the popular folklore, well before Lincoln ever figured out that modesty was a path to power.

The great irony, of course, is that the log-cabin-and-hard-cider slogan was much truer of Van Buren's life than his opponent's, and that he was being outsmarted by a ruthless opposition that had mastered all of his techniques. But no one was interested in the truth in 1840—only in the result. The Whigs had developed a national organization that was every bit as efficient as Van Buren's, and after learning from the outsider appeal of the early Jackson campaigns, they now saw an opportunity to steal some Democratic thunder.

It is impossible to list all the dramatic moments of the 1840 campaign, but it's clear that the election struck home with the electorate in a way that no previous election had. Perhaps it was the need to move beyond the Panic of 1837. Perhaps it was the greater suffrage that Van Buren himself had helped to usher in. Certainly, some of the zeal was contrived—in fact, most of it. But it was a movement all the same. The Whig strategists brilliantly stoked the fires of anti–Van Burenism. In May, Horace Greeley launched his paper the *Log Cabin*, which was soon selling eighty thousand copies weekly. Wild rumors spread about Van Buren, including outright lies that he was a closet Federalist, or that he had opposed the War of 1812, the very war that gave him his start. The charges grew nastier; one paper called him a "groveling demagogue" who had "slimed himself into the presidency." A typical speaker played on his Dutch heritage: "Nothing short of Omnipotence can save the little cabbage eater."

Giant parades were held, including one at the Whig convention in Baltimore that may have included as many as 75,000 people. Huge balls were rolled across the country to show Harrison's building momentum. Manufacturers churned out an endless supply of cheap trinkets, from "Tippecanoe Shaving Soap or Log-Cabin Emollient" to "Tippecanoe Tobacco." Liquor was especially prevalent in the hard-cider movement, and a new word entered the American vocabulary when the E.C. Booz Distillery of Philadelphia began to ship huge quantities of "Old Cabin Whiskey"—a.k.a. booze—in bottles shaped like log cabins. There was an undeniable sexual excitement to these frantic proceedings, and if women could not vote, they certainly came out in large numbers to laugh at their menfolk. Vice President Johnson was mortified, writing, "I am sorry to say that I have seen ladies joining in the [Whigs] and wearing ribands across their breast with two names printed on them."

Perhaps most effectively, a huge number of songs were written. The 1840 election might be as interesting to a musical as to a political historian. Greeley wrote with satisfaction, "Our songs are doing more good than anything else. . . . Really, I think every song is good for five hundred new subscribers." "Tippecanoe and Tyler Too" and "Van, Van, he's a used up man" are only two of hundreds, probably thousands of ditties that were spun out and forgotten during that overheated summer. One went: "Old Tip he wears a homespun coat / He has no ruffled shirt-wirt-wirt / But Mat he has the golden plate / And he's a little squirt-wirt-wirt." The latter noise was supposed to be made while spitting a jet of tobacco juice through one's teeth.

The Democrats did what they could, but they struggled from the start of the campaign to define themselves. When the party gathered in Baltimore in May to confirm its nominees, there was deep opposition to Richard Johnson as vice president from all quarters. Van Buren persevered in getting him through, but many party members were unhappy, including Andrew Jackson in Tennessee.

Once the campaign was under way, the Democrats tried their best, but they simply failed to match the enthusiasm of their opponents. Around the nation, orators defended Van Buren as the simple champion of democracy, or as "the pilot that weathered the storm!," the stout defender of "the sober second thought of the people." But the times demanded a more sophisticated response and a sexier slogan. He had none to offer. He certainly worked hard, and set an important precedent by giving obvious campaign speeches at ceremonial events around the country. For the first time, a president was striving openly for reelection, breaking a taboo that would remain in place until the early twentieth century.

The result, which came in November, was a foregone conclusion. Van Buren won only six states—Alabama, Arkansas, South Carolina, Virginia, Illinois, and New Hampshire—and New York was not one of them. The Whigs won the presidency and both Houses of Congress—in other words, everything. And they did it in impressive fashion, generating so much excitement that 80 percent of the voting population (all white males) cast ballots. Van Buren won 60 votes (1.1 million popular) to 234 for Harrison (1.3 million popular). The publicity machine they had built crowed its exultation, with headlines like "The Country Saved!" and "Van Burenism Lies Prostrate in the Dust," so much so that James Silk Buckingham was distressed for American democracy. He pondered the problem in his journal: "The language here used would induce any stranger to suppose that the party in power were absolute tyrants, ruling by virtue of divine right, and in no way responsible to the people; and the rebuking parties were democrats, and friends of liberty and free institutions. But the fact is just the reverse of this." Not for the first time, a candidate had been elected who bore little resemblance to the person described on handbills around the country.

John Quincy Adams may have been gratified by the result, but he, too, was disturbed by the way it had been achieved, through chicanery and cheap political slogans and unchecked hostility between the parties. He considered it a "revolution in the habits and manners of the people," and being an Adams, he worried about what it portended for the future. "Their manifest tendency is to civil war," he concluded glumly. Some—those who won—saw it as the vindication of democracy. But the tawdriness of this campaign, with its false claims and easy sound bites, signaled what Henry

Adams would later call the degradation of the democratic dogma. Out on the Illinois prairie, a young friend of Lincoln's, Albert T. Bledsoe, worried that "pandemonium had been let loose upon earth."

For all the noise and heat generated by the 1840 campaign, its most lasting legacy may have been one of the shortest words in the English language. In the spring of 1839, the phrase "OK" began to circulate in Boston as shorthand for "oll korrect," a slangy way of saying "all right." Early in 1840, Van Buren's supporters began to use the trendy expression as a way to identify their candidate, whom they labored to present as "Old Kinderhook," perhaps in imitation of Jackson's Old Hickory. Van Buren even wrote "OK" next to his signature. It spread like wildfire, and to this day it is a universal symbol of something elemental in the American character— informality, optimism, efficiency, call it what you will. It is spoken seven times a day by the average citizen, two billion utterances overall. And, of course, it goes well beyond our borders; if there is a single sound America has contributed to the esperanto of global communication, this is it. It is audible everywhere—in a taxicab in Paris, in a café in Istanbul, in the languid early seconds of the Beatles' "Revolution," when John Lennon steps up to the microphone and arrestingly calls the meeting to order. There are worse legacies that a defeated presidential candidate could claim.

After losing, Van Buren still had to deliver his final message to Congress. Jabez Hammond summed it up well at the time:

But, though defeated, Mr. Van Buren was not conquered. His last message contained a calm and dignified retrospect of his administration. He exhibited a clear view of our foreign relations, and showed them to be in a most happy, honorable and prosperous condition. He gave a history of the embarrassments which the government had been obliged to encounter, in consequence of the failure of the banks to perform their engagements. He insisted that the course he had recommended was the only one that could have been adopted, except that of incorporating a bank of the United States; he denounced that measure as unconstitutional, and as one which had been repeatedly repudiated by the people of the nation. He urged economy in the public expenditures; he showed that expenditures for ordinary purposes had been greatly diminished during his administration; he contended that the revenue of the government, without an increase of taxes, would be sufficient to defray all the necessary expenses; and he protested against the creation of a national debt. Although he left the enemy in possession of the field of battle, he himself retired from the arena in the spirit and with the dignity of a conqueror.

That was probably too generous a description. In truth, Van Buren *was* defeated, and badly. He would never hold elective office again; his career ended as prematurely as it had begun. The winds of fortune blow very strong in American politics. But despite a presidency that was disappointing in many ways, he could return to New York satisfied that he had remained true to his understanding of the Democracy, imperfect as that may have been, and that most others would have fared worse under the difficult circumstances he had faced. In fact, many were about to, as the United States entered the dreariest presidential season in its history, a twenty-year drought that did not end until the watershed of the 1860 election.

Van Buren shivered through the same damp inaugural ceremony that elevated and killed William Henry Harrison, and then made his way north, to the home state he had not lived in for twenty years. He arrived by ship at Manhattan, and found a surprise that must have warmed his jaded heart. A huge number of the city's poor came out in the rain to greet him, conscious that, for all his imperfections, this New Yorker had somewhere represented their interests in a government where they had precious few allies. There is no better way to describe the scene, and how deeply it must have moved Van Buren, than to quote from the sputtering remarks an angry Whig (George Templeton Strong) wrote in his diary, indignant at Van Buren and the leveling energy he still possessed, despite losing everything.

> March 23. Had to wait half an hour in the drizzle at the corner of Rector Street and Broadway while Matty's triumphal procession was going up. A disgusting assemblage of the unwashed democracy they were, generally speaking, a more rowdy, draggletailed, jailbird-resembling gang of truculent loafers than the majority of them I never witnessed before. Considering the rain, they turned out in force—and the rain, by the by, was a blessing to some of them, for the ablution was badly needed. Butler boys on horseback—there was an unlimited number of them. Carts with twenty little blackguards sticking to each, a dozen grand marshals with chapeaux and swords galloping about and getting into everybody's way in the intensity of their excitement, several very formidable brass bands, divers gorgeous banners, and so forth, with a great predominance of pedestrians from the neighborhood of the Points apparently, passed one; and then came the triumphal car, to wit, a shabby barouche and four with Matty himself, hat in hand, looking as happy as a man could be expected to in the rain without hat or umbrella. He looks older than I supposed.

8

Resurgemus

If Van Buren had lost America, he still owned New York, and he stayed in Manhattan for a few weeks after his tumultuous return, attending receptions and plays and upholding his penchant for high living. Appropriately, he also went to church, where he was again observed by the ubiquitous diarist George Templeton Strong:

> Matty Van Buren was there, in the pew of his brother president, Duer of Columbia College, and by a curious coincidence the subject of the sermon was the spiritual blessings that flow from retiracy and seclusion from the busy world and the cares of active life. If I wasn't nearsighted I've no doubt I should have observed Matty wince considerably.

Inevitably, Van Buren ran out of reasons to put off "retiracy," and so he finally wended his way up the Hudson to Kinderhook. He arrived there on May 8, 1841, setting off something like pandemonium, or as near to it as Dutch farmers could get. Early in the afternoon, a "numerous and respectable portion of the citizens" assembled at the steamboat wharf to receive their most famous son. When his boat came into view, an artillery piece began firing and did not stop until he reached the wharf, at which point the local brass band added to the din. A carriage hastily took him to the village, where cannons were fired, bells rung, and a series of long speeches offered to "a large assemblage" with "a goodly number of ladies." Finally, Van Buren took the rostrum and profusely thanked "the Democracy of my native county" for their welcome. He once again defended his fiscal policies, denying any regret, and insisting, in characteristically long sentences, that he would do it all exactly the same if he could. Following his speech, his old friend Benjamin Butler stood up and reminded the crowd of the unending series of adversities that Van Buren had stared down since his childhood in the small town that now turned out for him. It was, in the language of the day, "a spectacle which made the hearts of all present, of every party, throb with proud exultation."

From there it was on to Lindenwald, the large home on the outskirts of town that Van Buren, ever careful, had bought in 1839 in case the White House was no longer available. There must have been satisfaction in knowing that the house had originally belonged to the Van Ness family, one of the powerful clans that had tried to block Van Buren's rise. But perhaps that was also a source of lingering insecurity, judging by the frenzy with which he set out redecorating the place to better fit his questionable taste. Over the next decade, a handsome eighteenth-century dwelling was transformed into an ornate Venetian doge's palace, complete with a four-story loggia tower to survey the Van Buren lands and the visitors, who did not seem to be coming as frequently as one might have expected. While it was not quite the worst building of the nineteenth century, it demonstrated one of our most impressive traits as a people— the ability to disregard all rules of architectural propriety and build McMonuments to ourselves. Lindenwald fit squarely in the long continuum joining Monticello and Graceland.

Safely ensconced in his country seat, Van Buren now had to confront the same existential problem that so many ex-presidents have faced, before and since. How exactly does one fill up the time after having been retired by the people, a little too soon? As a relatively young ex-president at fifty-eight, he must have felt no little sense of dislocation. Like Rip Van Winkle, Van Buren was now awkwardly repatriated to the small village that he had fled all those years ago. How exotic he must have seemed to Kinderhook, and vice versa. At the beginning of 1841, he was directing a powerful economy, taking steps to avert foreign conflict, overseeing thousands of federal employees, and managing the affairs of a huge national party. A few months later, he was watching his potatoes grow and wondering about crop rotation.

Typically, Van Buren wasted little time on self-reflection, and threw himself into his new life as a rural squire—the role that all early American presidents claimed to love but which none except Washington actually sought. He worked the fields himself, improved his farmland by building dams and orchards, spoke Dutch with his old friends, and surprised the local farmers with his agricultural energy. At the same time, he maintained some of the habits he had formed in Washington, reading extensively, writing letters, and entertaining often (he spent about twice as much on butter, wine, and champagne as he did on taxes and church). Three of his four sons lived in close proximity, and a grandson was born that first summer on the farm. Van Buren claimed, perhaps sincerely, that he had "never spent as pleasant a summer."

Still, as he gazed at the prints of Jefferson and Jackson on his wall, Van Buren remained conscious that a new election was approaching in 1844, and that he might very well be the candidate again. It was encouraging that things were going badly for the Whigs— President Harrison had died a month after taking office, and President Tyler, a former Democrat, was distrusted on both sides of the aisle. Inevitably, Van Buren's thoughts turned to reclaiming what had been taken from him.

In the time-honored Van Buren tradition, he began his campaign with a journey, reminiscent of the long trips he had taken when orchestrating the creation of the Democratic Party. In early 1842, not even a year after his removal, Van Buren set out one more time from Kinderhook, determined to renew his acquaintance with the American people. It was an extraordinary pilgrimage, worthy of Ulysses, which exceeded all of his earlier ones, and included every region of what was by now a much bigger country. As usual, he started by heading toward the North Star of presidential politics— the South. From New York, he went to Philadelphia, Baltimore, and Charleston, the beginning of several weeks in South Carolina with allies and in-laws. From there he traveled overland through Georgia, Alabama, and Mississippi to New Orleans for the first time. Then it was up the Mississippi to Memphis, and across Tennessee to visit Jackson at his home, the Hermitage. It was a welcome reunion for the two old gamecocks, and Jackson was especially gratified that the Southwest could see Van Buren as he had seen him—"a plain man of middle size, plain and affable," not "a dwarf Dutchman" or "a little dandy who you might lift in a bandbox."

From the Jackson summit Van Buren headed through Kentucky, where he saw Clay, and into the Old Northwest, where he became the first current or former president to visit the rapidly growing city of Chicago. On his way there, in the middle of June 1842, poor roads forced him to stop in the small town of Rochester, Illinois, for one of the most memorable nights of his trip. A group of local officials, desperate to please Van Buren in this accidental location, brought along the funniest raconteur in the vicinity, overlooking the fact that his politics were all wrong (Whig), and that he had been acting erratically due to a severe personal crisis over whether to marry or not.

All evening, the young Abraham Lincoln and Martin Van Buren delighted each other with their stories. Van Buren took the crowd back to his earliest days in New York politics, when Hamilton and Burr circled each other. According to a lucky witness, Lincoln responded with an endless supply of stories, "one following another in rapid succession, each more irresistible than its predecessor. The fun continued until after midnight, and until the distinguished traveler insisted that his sides were sore from laughing." Van Buren later claimed that he had never "spent so agreeable a night in my life." That is no small claim from someone who had been listening to and telling the tallest tales in American politics for more than three decades. His early memories embraced long conversations with the founders, as he strained to inherit the mantle of their greatness. Now, in a very different role, he was able to see something of America's future as well. Lincoln, too, must have taken something from his first close encounter with the presidency. They could not have been more different—in their politics, their appearance, and their positions in the trajectory of life—and yet Lincoln and Van Buren shared a great deal as well. Their evening together, two ships passing in the prairie night, offers one of the more intriguing chance meetings in American history.

Van Buren finally returned home on July 28, 1842, having traveled more than seven thousand miles and shaken two hundred thousand hands. He had shored up his credentials, renewed his ties with local bosses, and emerged deeply energized by his contact with the far-flung American people. He was, in other words, a most obvious candidate for someone who still claimed, coyly, not to be a candidate. Soon, the old publicity mill he had created would bring out articles demanding his return. The *Democratic Review* even published a sonnet to him that bears notice, if only for the fact that it was the only work of poetry devoted to Van Buren until Ezra Pound developed his unlikely fascination a century later. "Fallen?," it began. "No, thou art not!," came the emphatic response.

But subtle changes in the political situation and in Van Buren himself indicated that the 1844 campaign would be different from the ones he had run before. The exuberance of the reception he had received in town after town emboldened him, and his time in the

Northwest deepened his aversion to slavery. In letters to his closest friends, a note of irritation toward the South began to creep in that had never been clearly stated before. Remembering the countless times he had thanklessly defended slavery and Indian removal, Van Buren now seemed to be recovering a lost anger that he had always suppressed in pursuit of his grand political strategy.

But the South, of course, was not inclined to let him off that easily. Calhoun also worked throughout 1843 to gain the nomination, renewing a rivalry that now stretched more than two decades. Even more dangerously, Texas came back into sharp focus in early 1844, forcing all candidates to declare whether they were for or against annexation, and by extension whether they wanted to alienate a huge swath of the North or the South. Again, Calhoun was at the center of things—as secretary of state under John Tyler, he had pressed hard for adding Texas to the South and the Union, in roughly that order.

There were a number of very good reasons to oppose taking Texas, despite our general belief today that American expansion was inevitable, virtuous, and foreordained. The United States had entered several prior treaties that recognized Mexico's sovereignty over Texas, and many experts felt that it was simply illegal to accept a disputed foreign province into the United States. Worse, it could lead to war. There was also a serious moral argument against annexation, in that it would reintroduce slavery where it no longer existed. Calhoun made no bones about it: he wanted Texas to come into the Union so that slavery, a positive good, might be extended and protected from British attempts to suppress it. This was a bitter pill for many Northerners to swallow—and the enormity of Texas also threatened to alter the delicate North-South balance in Congress.

Yet expansion was enormously popular among a people straining for largeness in everything they did. It was the catnip of the 1840s, perfectly captured by the electric phrase "Manifest Destiny," coined by Van Buren's protégé John Louis O'Sullivan. From the

Oregon territory to the Caribbean, Americans had an insatiable appetite for real estate, and a politician who failed to throw red meat out to the voters ran a real risk of being left behind. There was no doubt where Andrew Jackson stood on the great Texas question: he was foursquare behind it, and the publication of a letter stating that fact put a huge amount of pressure on Van Buren to once again follow Old Hickory.

By now the presumptive nominee, Van Buren had everything to gain and nothing to lose by issuing one of his famously noncommittal statements on Texas. Instead, he shocked political handicappers by stating in no uncertain terms that he was opposed to Texan annexation. In response to a query from a Mississippi congressman, William Hammet, Van Buren wrote out a reply on April 20 that reshaped the campaign and the known political universe for many years to come. Speaking a language that had not been heard before at the highest reaches of the Democratic Party, Van Buren argued that a naked land grab would harm America's reputation for "reason and justice" and would almost certainly bring war with Mexico. He did not foreclose on the future possibility of accepting Texas under the right circumstances, but he could not agree to it at present, with Calhoun turning the question into a referendum on slavery and imperfect information flowing from the White House. It was a brave decision, and his supporters were enormously gratified. Silas Wright, the conscience of the Northern Democracy, wrote that he had never "felt more proud."

His enemies were probably just as delighted. Immediately after the publication of the Hammet letter, Southerners let loose with a howl of "fever and fury" and claimed that it proved he had never been one of them. Henry Clay released a similar statement at the same time, but aroused far less anger. Van Buren's old friends in Virginia, where he had launched the great North-South alliance, rose up as one against him. James Buchanan, the boss of Pennsylvania, pronounced Van Buren "a dead cock in the pit." In fact, he had done precisely what so many of his critics had said he was incapable of doing: he had taken a strong stand on principle, aware that it might cost him the presidency—as in fact it did. Even later that spring, when he might have recanted, he refused, saying he would not trim "his sails to catch the passing breeze." This was Van Buren at his best.

Only a month after the Hammet letter was published, the Democracy met in Baltimore to anoint a candidate. Although they knew they were wounded, Van Buren's supporters still expected to prevail over a field of weaker candidates. They were not prepared for one of the sleaziest conventions in political history. Over a succession of very hot days in late May, it became clear that Van Buren's enemies had laid the groundwork for a palace revolt. While he commanded a majority of the delegates, he could not get to the necessary two-thirds, a rule that dated from the 1832 convention, infuriating the New Yorkers who saw the rule as anachronistic. Benjamin Butler became white with fury during a speech before the convention, stamping up and down to express his anger. But a large number of sordid promises had been made to neutral delegates, and Van Buren's friends could not get to the necessary number.

Instead, the crowd settled into the sickening rhythms of a deadlocked convention, each vote pulling early supporters away from Van Buren and toward newcomers who were willing to compromise on Texas and slavery. Enraged, the New Yorkers narrowly avoided fistfights with Southerners, and a number of harsh speeches were given that exposed the frightening fault lines beneath the party. Finally, Tennessee's James Polk, the former Speaker of the House and a friend of Jackson's, emerged as the original "dark horse" candidate. The convention tried to throw a sop to New York by offering the second spot to Silas Wright, but Wright, responding through the new technology of the telegraph, refused on principle. As Henry Thoreau would write, simply because the South and the North could now speak more quickly to each other did not mean that they had anything to say.

It would take a long time before the wounds of the 1844 convention were healed. Thomas Hart Benton, Van Buren's friend from Missouri, saw a dark design behind the scenes in Baltimore: "Disunion is at the bottom of this long-concealed Texas machination. Intrigue and speculation cooperate; but disunion is at the bottom; and I denounce it to the American people. Under the pretext of getting Texas into the Union, the scheme is to get the South out of it." Sixteen years later, many would agree with Benton's prescient analysis. The two-thirds rule would stay on the books until Franklin D. Roosevelt forcibly removed it in 1936, to the distress of Southern Democrats.

The Van Buren camp retired to lick its wounds. George Templeton Strong wrote that the ticket was "a severe dose for the Northern Democracy," and added, "if Van Buren would consent to run, as he certainly won't, I believe they'd be tempted to make a schism in the party." That, too, was a prescient remark, but Van Buren was not yet ready to abandon his party, even though it had abandoned him. Instead he worked hard to swing New York for Polk, and in a very close campaign, he managed to do just that—a result that was crucial to Polk's narrow victory. Expecting to be handsomely rewarded when it came time to select the new cabinet, Van Buren was devastated when Polk ignored all of his recommendations and instead favored a rival New York clique.

This was the last straw for many of Van Buren's friends, and the New York Democracy began to unravel. Van Buren's son John was especially angry and spoke loudly and frequently about settling scores. It was about politics—what wasn't?—but it also touched, as everything now did, on the slavery divide. When Polk led the United States into war against Mexico, winning an enormous amount of new territory, the shadows only deepened. As the New York party split into pro- and anti-slavery camps (loosely nicknamed Hunkers and Barnburners), tensions rose to a boiling point. At the 1847 state convention, a witness reported, "never was there a fiercer, more bitter and relentless conflict between the Narragansetts and the

Pequods than this memorable conflict between the Barnburners and the Hunkers."

It must have been an agonizing time for Van Buren. He had devoted his entire life to building the Democracy, first at the state level and then across the nation. But now the world looked very different. The South had sabotaged him at Baltimore. Polk had personally humiliated him. Jackson had died in 1845. And all those closest to Van Buren were heading in a radical new direction. John Van Buren was becoming a formidable leader in his own right, and a gifted orator in a way that his father never was, "enthusiastic, frank, bold, and given to wit." He began to call for mass meetings of the Barnburners, a first step to declaring war on the Hunkers. His father wrote a King Lear letter to a friend, trying to stop the dissolution of the party he had built. But the old warrior could not help answering the summons to battle.

At the beginning of 1848, Van Buren moved to a hotel in New York's Washington Square and worked on a lengthy manuscript outlining his position. There, where so many literary manifestos would be issued in the twentieth century, he wrote out the "Barnburner Manifesto." It demanded that the national party recognize the Barnburners as the legitimate representatives of New York Democracy, and supported a ban on slavery in the newly acquired territory from Mexico. Even more than that, it looked searchingly into early American history and found no evidence that the founders intended to expand slavery, or to protect it beyond where it existed. This was a powerful argument from a former president, and constituted a worthy, unjustly neglected precursor to Lincoln's Cooper Union Address. The manifesto quickly created a sensation in New York, and John Van Buren wrote his father asking if he would consider running for president as the candidate of a new party. Van Buren's response, on May 3, revealed all the currents and countercurrents flowing inside of him, calling for party loyalty, but proud that his son wanted him to bear the standard of the new organization he was building.

These contradictions were entirely in keeping with the moment; 1848 was an annus mirabilis, one of those rare years when the world turns upside down and anything under the sun feels possible. Across the Atlantic, a revolution in France was bringing the established order to its knees and hinted at even greater things to come—the spread of democracy across Europe, and the abolition of slavery around the world. But that was hardly the only event dazzling newspaper readers. In the United States, dramatic events were leading to the close of the Mexican War, and a roiling debate was forming over how to shape the peace. The discovery of gold in California, one of the newly acquired territories, only increased the din. Politicians from all backgrounds were acting very strangely. Abraham Lincoln, an obscure first-term congressman from Illinois, committed a form of hara-kiri by denouncing Polk for his aggression, and challenging him to show the precise spot where Mexicans had originally attacked Americans. For years afterward, Illinois voters would deride the man they called "Spotty" Lincoln.

In this disorienting context, the creation of a third party no longer seemed anathema. And so Van Buren moved inexorably toward a fateful decision, half pulled by his son, half pushed by his disgust with the way inferior politicians were ruining the great party that he had built. After the national Democratic convention accepted New York's Hunker delegation in May, the Barnburners stormed out and John Van Buren called for a convention of their own in Utica. Inevitably, the question approached: would Martin Van Buren run one more time for the presidency? In response, he drafted a nineteen-page letter on June 20 answering no, but indicating by his detailed answer that he was interested. In stronger language than he had previously used, he outlined the long history of Congress's efforts to constrain slavery, which was utterly at odds with "the principles of the Revolution." He now went beyond his previous position by claiming that Congress had the power to limit its spread—a crucial point—and that having the power, it should use it. Thrilled by this bracing declaration of principles, the Utica convention nominated Van Buren and he was once again off to the races.

Official Washington was horrified at the news. Polk denounced the new party as "more threatening to the Union" than anything since the Hartford convention. Calhoun called Van Buren's letter to Utica "the fierce war-cry of a new and formidable party," and identified its author as "a bold, unscrupulous and vindictive demagogue." Undeterred, the Barnburners held an even larger gathering in Buffalo on August 9, attracting twenty thousand people in a motley assemblage that combined former Whigs and Northern Democrats. The vice presidential nomination went to Charles Francis Adams, the son of Van Buren's old rival John Quincy Adams, who had died on the floor of Congress in February. The resulting platform had a little bit for everyone—economic opportunity and cheap land for old Jacksonians, tariffs and improvements for old Whigs, and an exuberant celebration of "Free Soil, Free Speech, Free Labor, and Free Men!" No longer would the Van Burenites have to apologize for gag rules, slave markets, and other insults to human liberty. Of course, no longer would they win elections, either.

The result was a foregone conclusion, but still it was interesting. It may be true, as William Allen Butler wrote, that "Van Buren's name was in it, but not his head or his heart." But once again he did his duty. Not only did he attack the new outrages of the Slave Power, but he argued movingly that "the wealth and power of a country consist in its labor." With his strange new bedfellows, Van Buren threw himself into the Free Soil campaign, writing letters across the country from Kinderhook. He never quite solved the problem that he was too moderate for some and too radical for others, but the campaign spread and, in so doing, laid a foundation for the Republican Party.

Predictably, the people who had always hated him let fly with all the weapons in their arsenal. Polk called him "the most fallen man" he had ever known. Daniel Webster thought it hilarious that "the leader of the Free Spoil party should have so suddenly become the leader of the Free Soil party." Newspapers denounced him as "the traitor and the hypocrite, the Judas Iscariot of the nineteenth century." But others saw something noble in the spectacle. Charles Sumner, who hardly would have defended the old Van Buren, admired "the Van Buren of to-day,—the veteran statesman, sagacious, determined, experienced, who at an age when most men are rejoicing to put off their armor girds himself anew, and enters the lists as the champion of freedom."

For a moment, a few exuberant supporters thought that it was possible the election would be thrown into the House and that Van Buren might prevail. But the actual numbers told otherwise. Van Buren received an impressive 291,804 votes—10 percent of the total—but he won no states outright. Gratifyingly, he tilted the election from the odious Lewis Cass, a conservative Michigan Democrat complicit in Van Buren's defeat at Baltimore in 1844, to the Whig general Zachary Taylor. (Taylor won 163 electoral votes and 1.36 million popular votes to 127 and 1.22 million for Cass.) That was a more than respectable performance, especially given that the Free Soil party could not get on the ballot in the South, with the exception of Virginia, where Van Buren won a grand total of nine votes. When some of his supporters claimed fraud, a Virginian answered memorably: "Yes Fraud! And we're still looking for the son-of-a-bitch who voted nine times."

Still, he had made history one more time. The Free Soil campaign was America's first great third-party effort. In one sense, it resembled a modern election—specifically the great Bull Moose campaign that a disgusted Theodore Roosevelt led in 1912, but also the single-issue grievances that have increasingly become a feature of modern presidential politics (Ross Perot, Ralph Nader). But it helps also to look retrospectively, and to see it as a final skirmish in the long fight that Van Buren had been waging for thirty years against Calhoun, since the day when Calhoun was the first official to pay him a visit in Washington. Certainly, there were more extreme Northerners and Southerners than Van Buren and Calhoun, but somehow the battle lines always seemed to be drawn around the personal rivalry between these two headstrong generals.

In the immediate aftermath of 1848, the young poet Walt Whitman, just finding his voice, wrote a poem entitled "Resurgemus" that gave vent to the extraordinary emotional energy he was feeling as one political world ended and a new one began to rise up around him. Whitman, a Van Buren supporter, was thrilled by the overthrow of kings across Europe during the revolutionary spring of 1848. But he also seethed with a barely containable rage at the insults to democracy that he saw all around him in the United States, beginning with the Slave Power and the politicians who would stop at nothing to advance human bondage. "Resurgemus"— Latin for "we will rise again"—expressed the frustrations of tens of thousands of Northern Democrats who sought an America consistent with the Declaration of Independence, and were no longer willing to accept meekly the verdicts of the Southern barons who controlled Congress. From Whitman: "O hope and faith! O aching close of exiled patriots' lives! O many a sicken'd heart! Turn back unto this day, and make yourselves afresh. And you, paid to defile the People! you liars, mark!" Frighteningly, he foresaw the corpses of young men and gave the reader a premonition of the Civil War. But the poem ends with a sense of hope far more powerful than its despair:

> Liberty! let others despair of you! I never despair of you.
> Is the house shut? Is the master away?
> Nevertheless, be ready—be not weary of watching;
> He will soon return—his messengers come anon.

It took an extraordinary anger to pry Van Buren loose from his deep devotion to party loyalty, and he never won back some of his old supporters. But slavery was an extraordinary evil, spreading in

1848 as it never had done, in complete contradiction to what seemed like the rising tide of human liberty elsewhere. Was Van Buren right to break with the Democracy and wage a quixotic campaign that was doomed to failure? Certainly it compromised his legacy as the standard-bearer of party discipline. But what better answer to the charges that he was more concerned with his advancement than with questions of principle? Van Buren's determination to rise again against his tormentors served notice that the once-careful Dutchman and thousands with him would no longer brook interference with the right of Americans to self-determination. That righteous rage would express itself, soon enough, in the great military struggle to eliminate slavery forever on the North American continent. If "Resurgemus" contained the seeds of *Leaves of Grass*, the startling poem that would revolutionize poetry in 1855, then Van Buren's last campaign contained the seeds of the epic war to determine America's character once and for all along the lines promised by the founders.

9

Oblivion

Life continued after 1848, of course. But for the first time in his life, Van Buren had no political campaigns ahead of him. So he settled down to a long retirement—this time for real—enjoying friends, family, and the dwindling numbers of visitors who beat a path to Lindenwald. If the White House receded ever further from his grasp, there was some consolation in the fact that he did not have to preside over the steady disintegration of the United States in the 1850s. It must have depressed him to watch the fissures between North and South widen to the point where no up-and-coming Martin Van Buren could hope to repair the damage.

Van Buren could also take comfort in his remarkable longevity—although one wonders if he found it a blessing or a curse. He had enjoyed fine wine and food all his life, but now, improbably, he was outliving all of his peers, including his many tormentors and the parade of mediocrities who inherited the presidency from him. Harrison, of course, died almost as soon as the office hit him in 1841. A number of chief magistrates succumbed soon after: Jackson in 1845, Adams in 1848, Polk in 1849, and Taylor in 1850. Calhoun exited in 1850, Clay and Webster in 1852. Throughout the decade before the Civil War, Van Buren enjoyed seniority among the ex-presidents, ultimately resembling one of the elderly patriarchs invented by Faulkner, who outlives first his own cohort, then his children's, until no one is quite sure who he was in the first place.

For all his pretended rusticity, Van Buren was incapable of inactivity, and if he was unable to reshape the country, then he continued to mold Lindenwald to his peculiar taste. The farmers of Kinderhook must have been shocked when he introduced the radical concept of the indoor toilet, and visitors to this day can see how elaborate that contraption must have seemed when it was installed with great ceremony inside the mansion. Van Buren kept current with politics, thanks to his newspapers and informants, but after the epic struggle of 1848 he retreated, as if chagrined by the boldness he had displayed in challenging the Democratic orthodoxy. He came back into the fold, supported the 1850 compromise engineered by his friend Henry Clay, and stood with the party again in 1852, even though it had hardly cleansed itself of its pro-slavery acolytes. Throughout the 1850s, as the crisis intensified, Van Buren generally approved the moderate position associated with younger politicians like Stephen Douglas—appalled by slavery, but reluctant to attack it in the bolder language being used by former Free Soilers as they assembled under the new banner of the Republican Party. Van Buren had only so much revolution in him. In 1858 he told a visitor, "I have nothing to modify or change. The end of slavery will come—amid terrible convulsion, I fear, but it will come."

In fairness, he had other problems on his mind. His four sons still occupied much of his time, not always happily. At a time in his life when he might have expected dependency to flow in the other direction, he was often called upon to support them. Smith Van Buren had moved to Lindenwald with his three children in 1849, as his wife lay dying of consumption, and oversaw the extensive renovations to the house performed by Richard Upjohn. Young Martin, who had served his father faithfully as a private secretary for years, now gave signs of a health crisis that would require serious medical attention and extensive, even desperate, travel to foreign climates.

For all his talents, John Van Buren never overcame his private demons, and though he was mentioned as a candidate for vice president in 1852, his support generally eroded among a welter of rumors about his taste for nightlife.

Van Buren remained a pillar of strength to those around him. The diarist Philip Hone likened his face to "the unruffled surface of a majestic river, which covers rocks and whirlpools, but shows no marks of agitation beneath." That imperturbability—so useful throughout his career in the cauldron of democracy—was confirmed by a small cluster of daguerreotypes he sat for in his declining years. The technology had appeared during his presidency, and now he allowed it to capture him for the ages. While a certain stolid fortitude was always evident in Van Buren portraiture, the images of the 1850s indicate an increasingly spectral figure, a cherubic face surrounded by wisps of white hair, including sideburns that never seemed to stop growing. Herman Melville, whose brother had been a leading supporter of Van Buren, never lost his fear that photography robbed something from the soul—to sit for a photograph, in his opinion, was to be "oblivionated." These final images of Van Buren, fading like a negative exposed to daylight, suggest that Melville was on to something.

But before oblivion settled upon him, he had some final business to attend to.

Van Buren had always enjoyed history—his obsession with Jefferson and strong memories of Hamilton and Burr show that he felt himself to be part of a continuum of sorts—and now that he had time on his hands, he began to look to history again for consolation. When his old friend Thomas Hart Benton, the fiery senator from Missouri, began to write his magnificent *Thirty Years' View*— arguably the finest political memoir ever written in this country— Van Buren helped considerably with his comments and recollections. When Alexander Hamilton's son John undertook an ambitious biography of his father, he came to Van Buren for help sorting through Hamilton's career in New York politics and his tortured relationship with Jefferson. In the 1850s, as the Constitution came under intense scrutiny for its intentions regarding slavery, Van Buren was increasingly looked to as a rare person with immediate recollections of the giants who built the nation. Finally, after years of insecurity about his educational attainments, he had become the Sage of Lindenwald.

Inevitably, these thoughts about history turned to the complicated question of his own mortality, and how he wished to be remembered. The past was everywhere in Kinderhook, and an obscure history of the town records that Van Buren spent noticeable time in local cemeteries, visiting in particular the grave of a woman he had once loved: "There is an abiding tradition of the grave of yet another, in a private burial plot three miles from the village, which he was wont to visit occasionally and stand reverently beside it with hat in hand." The same history offers a tantalizing morsel about his personal life as well: "Some of us know of one of Kinderhook's estimable and cultivated women who declined to marry the ex-President." Her name and story are, alas, lost to the historical record.*

To keep his own story from disappearing, and to achieve the peculiar immortality we reserve for the writers of very long books that are never checked out of the library, Van Buren turned to the great challenge of writing his autobiography. Jabez Hammond, the historian of New York politics, presciently urged him to describe things "as they *were* not as they *ought* to have been"—good advice for us all. He commenced the project in earnest in 1854, as he traveled around Europe with his sick son, Martin. It would have been difficult to find a more unlikely place to begin than Sorrento, where the tiny ex-presidential entourage arrived in June of 1854—but maybe Sorrento's distance from Kinderhook was exactly what opened the floodgates of his memory. Once the words came, they came in a torrent, written hastily in his unreadable handwriting,

*She was likely Margaret Silvester, the spinster daughter of his first employer.

and describing the thousands of political calculations that had propelled his career forward in the early days of the republic. The autobiography would occupy him for years, along with his history of political parties—a subject that was close to his heart. Although he never exactly finished the memoir (to do so would be to admit the end was near, as Ulysses Grant proved when he expired upon completing his manuscript), he poured considerable energy into the effort. The result was a wandering account that focused too much on some episodes (his embassy to England) and too little on others (how he formed the party, how he sabotaged Calhoun, his presidency), but provided fascinating insights into the period.

Van Buren wrote another valedictory of sorts in 1858 when he composed a solicitous, twenty-page letter to his son John about his political prospects. Although John's fortunes were on the wane, Van Buren had limitless hopes for him and urged him to take a series of steps that would put him in a favorable position for the presidency. The letter is fascinating to read not only to see Van Buren as a parent (and a rather delusional one, given the unlikelihood of John's ascent) but also to glimpse the ambition that had powered his own difficult rise to the summit. He insisted on the great value of hard work for any successful candidate, and the importance, paradoxically, of not appearing to be trying too hard for the post. In what must have been a self-reflective comment, he warned him strenuously against becoming a "professional" politician: "There is no 'one' in whose pockets the people are so prone to pour lead, as a man who pursues politics for a living. They soon come to regard him as a wanton upon Providence, and are constantly disposed to show him the cold shoulder. Although many make their living by it, they get it by hook or crook, and no public honors sit well upon them." Finally, he urged him to stay away from the petty deals over patronage that had occupied so much of his own time. With the voice of a seasoned politician, he wrote his son: "None of these things pay in any way. Seven out of ten of those you benefit will prove ungrateful, all of your opponents will be vindictive, you will fritter away your strength, and worry yourself to no purpose by caring about, and still more by meddling in any of these matters."

That same year, he was thrown from a galloping horse, but he emerged from the accident unscathed. The veteran of more than one tussle wrote a friend, "Does this not speak well of my skull?" The Civil War was another body blow, but Van Buren accepted it with the equanimity that had distinguished his entire career. He used all of his influence to prevent the secession of the Southern states, voiced some anti-extremist opinions directed to both sides, and proposed a constitutional convention as a last resort. But when push came to shove, this lifelong disciple of Jeffersonian democracy and lover of the South stood unwaveringly by Abraham Lincoln and the Union. When Franklin Pierce asked Van Buren to lead a meeting of ex-presidents to call for peace, Van Buren smelled dis-union and would have none of it. Before a worried group of Kinder-hook burghers, he gave his clear opinion: "The attack upon our flag and the capture of Fort Sumter by the Secessionists could be regarded in no other light than as the commencement of a treason-able attempt to overthrow the Federal Government by military force." His call to the New York Democracy to support Lincoln came at an important time, and did not go unappreciated by the beleaguered new president.

When Walt Whitman, walking down Broadway one April evening in 1861, heard that war had broken out, he was so stunned that he resolved to drink only water and milk, as if his constitution was somehow tied to the nation's. Similarly, Van Buren's health declined rapidly with the onset of hostilities. He lingered into the war's second year, and then expired at 2 a.m. on July 24, 1862, a day and a half after Lincoln read the first draft of his Emancipation Proclamation to a startled cabinet. Van Buren could hardly have chosen his entrance and exit more dramatically. Born to the Revolution that created this country, he died a casualty of the Civil War that nearly destroyed it. One hopes that he knew the Union would prevail, and there is much in his optimistic life to suggest that he would have taken such a view, but it is impossible to say with certainty.

Lincoln returned the favor of Van Buren's support with a more than gracious statement of presidential sorrow over the departure of his predecessor:

> Washington, July 25, 1862
> The President with deep regret announces to the people of the United States the decease, at Kinderhook, N.Y., on the 24th Instant, of his honored predecessor Martin Van Buren.
>
> This event will occasion mourning in the nation for the loss of a citizen and a public servant whose memory will be gratefully cherished. Although it has occurred at a time when his country is afflicted with division and civil war, the grief of his patriotic friends will measurably be assuaged by the consciousness that while suffering with disease and seeing his end approaching his prayers were for the restoration of the authority of the Government of which he had been the head and for peace and good will among his fellow-citizens.

Lincoln then ordered the ceremonial rituals, which again exceeded what might have been expected. The entire government, save the military, closed the next day, and flags were displayed at half-staff. At dawn thirteen guns were fired, and then a single gun every thirty minutes until sunset, when thirty-four guns were fired, in tribute to all of the United States, including those in rebellion. Van Buren would have appreciated that. For six months following his death, through some of the bloodiest fighting of the war (Second Bull Run, Antietam, Fredericksburg), all officers in the U.S. Army and Navy wore black crape on their left arms in tribute to the eighth president. Thus Abraham Lincoln completed the unlikely friendship that had begun that night on the prairie in 1842 when he and Van Buren had told uproarious political stories late into the night.

If Kinderhook had ignored Van Buren on his way up, it corrected the mistake on his way out. The funeral was the grandest event in the history of the town. Services were held first at Lindenwald and then in the village church where his ancestors had worshipped. According to the local paper, thousands stood outside. His pall-bearers were fourteen friends from Kinderhook, most with Dutch patronyms. After a series of sermons, the "thronging multitude" passed the casket before it was taken away in a procession led by Engine Company No. 2, including eighty-one carriages and an end-less line of political dignitaries, clerics, and the small fry Van Buren would have appreciated the most.

There the story might have ended, except for the fact that Van Buren refused to die. Long after his demise, his publishing career followed a strange logic of its own. In 1867, five years after the funeral, his first book was published, the *Inquiry into the Origin and Course of Political Parties in the United States*. It is a learned work, deeply immersed in the rivalry between Jefferson and Hamilton, but less forthright about the struggles of his own generation. Fifty-three years later, in 1920, the companion volume appeared, his long-awaited *Autobiography of Martin Van Buren*. It was not exactly a book to launch the Jazz Age, but the miracle is perhaps that it made it into print at all.

His biographies appeared equally erratically. First out of the box was a sensitive short portrait by William Allen Butler, the son of Van Buren's old partner, entitled *Martin Van Buren: Lawyer, Statesman and Man* (1862). But even at a moment when one might have expected interest in the just-departed president, Butler confessed that "he goes unnoticed." Twenty-seven years later (1889), at the end of a very long life, the great nineteenth-century historian George Bancroft added another volume to the pile when he wrote *Martin Van Buren to the End of His Public Career*. From the unentic-ing title to the book's timing, it was a spectacularly bad idea. What vestigial debt, lost to memory, was Bancroft trying to pay? He must have known that no one would read it, but he wrote it anyway, fulfilling an old promise to the Democratic chieftain, and perhaps to himself as well. The 1930s saw a brief resurgence of interest—perhaps because of the Depression, the New Deal, and curiosity about antecedents to the great coalition FDR was building. In 1945, Arthur Schlesinger Jr.'s *The Age of Jackson* paid serious attention to Van Buren, tying Jackson to Roosevelt and Van Buren to both. But to this day, there have been sufficiently few biographies of Martin Van Buren that a reader with time on his hands (and what other kind of Van Buren acolyte is there?) can reasonably expect to read every work on Van Buren ever written—something that would be impossible to say about the other giants of the early republic.

Van Buren lived as well in the memories of his younger friends in politics. A number of former Democrats and Van Buren Free Soilers populated Lincoln's inner circle, including the Blairs (Frank and Montgomery), Gideon Welles, and Vice President Hannibal Hamlin. Perhaps his most direct heir was Samuel Tilden, a young man he had helped and who became one of his closest friends. Tilden, no mean politician in his own right, became the governor of New York and the Democratic candidate for president in 1876. That bitterly contested election, which in many ways presaged the turmoil of 2000, ended in agonizing defeat for Tilden after a highly partisan commission awarded contested votes from Florida, Louisiana, South Carolina, and Oregon to Rutherford B. Hayes (Tilden won the popular vote by 250,000). One suspects that if Van Buren had been there to count the votes, the election might have turned out differently. Tilden went on to amass a great fortune, most of which he left to what became the New York Public Library. That irreplaceable edifice remains a tribute not only to Tilden but to the political mentor who discovered him. Van Buren always had an eye for young talent.

Van Buren also lived on, as all presidents do, in the world of gossip, innuendo, and half-truth that lurk in the shadows behind any important leader, especially one who disturbs the status quo. Near the end of his life, at the end of the nineteenth century, Walt Whitman remembered Van Buren fondly as a "brilliant manager," though not quite Lincolnesque. He also added the confused recollection that John Van Buren was the illegitimate son of Aaron Burr. Nor was Whitman the only poet who dilated on the eighth president. Improbably, well into the twentieth century the great modernist Ezra Pound developed a literary crush on Van Buren, in one of the strangest artist-muse relationships in the history of creative expression. "Canto 37" of his *Seventy Cantos* is a long-winded poetic exploration of the issues surrounding the Panic of 1837, with some sections drawing upon Van Buren's autobiography (written "in the vicinage of Vesuvius, in the mirror of memory"). It ends with an ecstatic Latinate celebration of the man Pound considered the author of economic freedom in America: "HIC JACET FISCI LIBERATOR" (here lies the liberator of money). Pound also wrote elsewhere that Van Buren was a "national hero" offering one of the "few clean and decent pages" in the history of the United States.

It is hard to say whether Pound's advocacy helped or hurt Van Buren. It is safe to say that there were not many other modernist poets clamoring to defend him, or to attack him for that matter, and any attention helped. But Pound's later zeal for Benito Mussolini did not do much to promote his reputation as a shrewd judge of character. In fact, his emotional embrace of Van Buren may have helped Pound more than it helped anyone else, because it offered convincing proof, as his defenders later claimed, that the poet was completely insane.

Finally, Van Buren lived on in the world where he was most comfortable: the political realm. Though his specific deeds were soon forgotten, the same battles he fought were repeated again and again over the course of the nineteenth and twentieth centuries. In every generation, champions of the people fought against the encroachments of corporations and malefactors of great wealth, and through most of these struggles, the modern Democratic Party that Van Buren had invented was a crucial instrument in the struggle. Franz Kafka, in his essay "The Great Wall of China," described a man-made structure so extensive and piecemeal that it could never be finished, and would require generations to complete, by which time the original plans would have been altered beyond recognition. Martin Van Buren's party shares a few of those characteristics.

Sometimes the echoes were more audible, and sometimes they were less. Certainly there were similitudes joining Van Buren and some of his more prominent successors. He was distantly related to the only other Dutch-American presidents, Theodore and Franklin Roosevelt, and shared a bit of common experience with them as well. Like Theodore Roosevelt, he was willing to run against the party he embodied as a third-party candidate when principles required it. And like Franklin Roosevelt, he assembled a vast national alliance of local interests, rooted especially in the Northeast and South, that restrained Wall Street, defended the disenfranchised, and infuriated his wealthy neighbors along the Hudson. It is worth remembering that for all his greatness, FDR also compromised heavily with the South to get his program through, and both of these careful Dutchmen frustrated friends as well as enemies with their mixture of amiability and emotional distance. True, the New Deal was built on a scale that was inconceivable to Van Buren, and FDR was a star of an entirely different magnitude, but there is something to be said for the comparison.

Once you start these ahistorical presidential comparisons, it is of course difficult to stop. Different similitudes join Van Buren to Kennedy (his fellow ethnic), to Lyndon Johnson (who wanted to build a vast Democratic Party "from the courthouse to the White House"), and to Clinton, who excited great vicissitudes of loyalty and animosity, but held together a diverse party as the economy changed dramatically. All of these democratic champions, like Van Buren, excited irrational hostility in radical fringes of the business community and much of this dislike translated into sensational gossip, like the rumors of Parisian elegance that had once hung like perfume over Van Buren. Cynically, this gossip often celebrated the luxury in which these friends of the people lived—a political lie that never fails to succeed, no matter how obvious the exaggeration, but which degrades democracy all the same. The 1840 anti–Van Buren campaign was so successful in its bombast and distortion that we have never entirely recovered.

But if our culture is amnesiac, forgetting crucial dates and places as soon as they are taught, it also spits people up when we least expect them. America continues to regurgitate Van Buren in the most unlikely places. In the debates over the League of Nations, an arch-Republican, Henry Cabot Lodge, quoted Van Buren when he argued that we should go to war only after a "sober second thought." When Pauline Esther Friedman wanted to write an advice column for the *San Francisco Chronicle* in 1956, she adopted the name "Abigail Van Buren" because she thought it sounded prestigious, and soon "Dear Abby" was a national institution. How Van Buren would have loved the irony that his poor name—so maligned by the grandees of the Hudson Valley—suggested the whiff of grandeur to a young social climber! In the 1988 campaign, Garry Trudeau drew a series of *Doonesbury* cartoons ridiculing George H. W. Bush (seeking to become the first vice president elected since 1836) and Yale's Skull and Bones Society as would-be grave robbers of Van Buren's tomb. Rumors persist that Van Buren's skull is, in fact, incarcerated there, along with those of Geronimo and Pancho Villa. If so, he is in good company, for to men of a certain privileged class, the architect of Democracy was as fearsome an opponent as any warrior on the battlefield.

Despite these blips on the radar screen, Van Buren will remain one of our lesser-known presidents, for reasons that he would understand. His presidency produced no lasting monument of social legislation, sustained several disastrous reverses, and ended with ignominious defeat after one short term. There will never be an animatronic Van Buren entertaining children at Disneyland alongside Abraham Lincoln. But still, he lives wherever people find gated communities shut to them. He lives particularly in the places far from the presidential stage where democracy does its best work—in the back rooms of union halls, fire stations, immigrant social clubs, granges, and taverns like the one he grew up in. Or even far from American shores, where courageous men and women are risking their lives every day to form opposition parties against the wishes of their governments.

He does not need fame, or pity, but Martin Van Buren is worthy of a sober second thought. Quite simply, it's antidemocratic to expect all of our leaders to be great, or to pretend that they are once they are in office and using the trappings of the presidency for theatrical effect. It goes without saying that we need our Lincolns and Washingtons—the United States would not exist without them. But we need our Van Burens, too—the schemers and sharps working to defend people from all backgrounds against their natural predators. For democracy to stay realistic, we need to remain realistic about our leaders and what they can and cannot do. In other words, we need books about the not-quite-heroic. Van Buren is history, and this book has reached its terminus, but, as Kafka tells us, the work is never done.

Perhaps it is best to give the last word to Harry Truman, another tough pol who followed a greater man as president, but who did a great deal behind the scenes to deepen the democracy that he loved—democracy with both a small and a big D. In the dark days of 1947, with the Cold War threatening to undo everything that all of his predecessors had worked toward, Truman saw the ghost of Martin Van Buren and drew some comfort from the fact that he was not alone. That night (January 6), he wrote a note in his diary, only recently discovered, remembering the little presidents as well as the greats, and urging all of us to treat those who hold the world's hardest office with the forbearance they deserve:

The floors pop and crack all night long. Anyone with imagination can see old Jim Buchanan walking up and down and worrying about conditions not of his making. Then there's Van Buren who inherited a terrible mess from his predecessor as did poor old James Madison. Of course Andrew Johnson was the worst mistreated of any of them. But they all walk up and down the halls of this place and moan about what they should have done and didn't. So—you see. I've only named a few. The ones who had Boswells and New England historians are too busy trying to control heaven and hell to come back here. So the tortured souls who were and are misrepresented in history are the ones who come back. It's a hell of a place.

Milestones

December 5, 1782   Martin Van Buren born in his father's tavern in Kinderhook, New York

1796   Van Buren begins apprenticeship with Francis Silvester

1798   Silvester family pressures Van Buren to join Federalist Party, but he refuses

1801   Van Buren moves to New York and into Aaron Burr's circle

1803   Van Buren gains admission to bar

1804   Van Buren refuses to vote for Burr for governor, but helps defend William Van Ness, Burr's second, after the Hamilton duel

1807   Van Buren marries Hannah Hoes in Catskill, New York

1808   Van Buren receives first political appointment as surrogate of Columbia County
Van Buren moves to Hudson, New York, and opens law practice

1812   Van Buren narrowly wins election as state senator

1813   Van Buren helps to found the *Albany Argus*

1814   Van Buren's Classification bill proposes that New York draft 12,000 men to aid in the war effort

1815   Van Buren becomes attorney general of New York

1817–21   Van Buren organizes "the Bucktails," later known as the Regency, a group of allies opposed to De Witt Clinton and sympathetic to Jeffersonian democracy

1819   Death of Hannah Van Buren
Van Buren removed as attorney general by Clintonians
Proposed admission of Missouri opens debate over future of slavery in which many friends of Van Buren play an active role

1821   New York Constitutional Convention expands suffrage and reforms patronage and judiciary
Van Buren elected to U.S. Senate and moves to Washington, D.C.

1823   Van Buren forms alliance with Thomas Ritchie, leader of the Richmond Junto

1824   Van Buren meets Thomas Jefferson at Monticello
       Van Buren supports presidential aspirations of William H. Craw-
       ford of Georgia; John Quincy Adams elected president of House
       of Representatives
1825   Erie Canal completed
1826–28   Van Buren organizes what will be known as the Democracy,
       or Democratic Party, through travel, correspondence, and the cre-
       ation of a national organization of coordinated regional alliances
       behind the presidential candidacy of Andrew Jackson
1827   Van Buren reelected to the U.S. Senate
1828   Tariff of Abominations raises tensions between North and South;
       Calhoun explores doctrine of nullification
       Jackson elected president and Van Buren elected governor of
       New York
January 1829   Van Buren inaugurated as governor
March 1829   Jackson inaugurated as president; Van Buren joins Jackson
       as secretary of state
1829   Eaton affair exposes factions in the cabinet; Van Buren sides with
       Eaton against Calhoun
December 1829   Jackson privately designates Van Buren his successor
1829–31   Van Buren serves as secretary of state; secures reciprocal trade
       agreement from Great Britain in Caribbean, indemnity payment
       from France, treaty with Ottoman Empire
1830   Van Buren offers conciliatory toast at Jefferson Day dinner fol-
       lowing hostile exchange between Jackson and Calhoun
       Van Buren helps Jackson prepare Maysville Road veto, delineat-
       ing limits to federal support for internal improvements
1831   Van Buren nominated as minister to England and sails for London
       Nat Turner Rebellion and founding of *The Liberator* in Boston
       raise tensions over slavery
1832   Calhoun kills Van Buren's nomination in the Senate
       Struggle to renew charter of the Bank of the United States
       Van Buren nominated at first Democratic Convention and
       elected as vice president for Jackson's second term
1833   Jackson and Van Buren tour northeastern states
1835   Van Buren nominated as presidential candidate at Democratic
       Party's Baltimore convention; Richard M. Johnson nominated as
       vice president
1836   Specie Circular
       Pinckney Gag Rule passes House
       Texas declares independence from Mexico
       Van Buren elected president

1837   Jackson recognizes the Texas Republic on the last day of his presidency

March 4, 1837   Van Buren inaugurated as eighth president

May 1837   The Panic of 1837 reaches peak intensity as New York banks close

May 15, 1837   Van Buren calls special session of Congress to address Panic

1837   First issue of the *United States Magazine and Democratic Review*

Abolitionist printer Elisha P. Lovejoy murdered in Alton, Illinois

British burn an American vessel, the *Caroline*, they suspect of running supplies to Canadian rebels

1838   John Quincy Adams presents 350 anti-slavery petitions to Congress

U.S. Exploring Expedition, commanded by Lt. Charles Wilkes, departs Norfolk, Virginia (returns 1842)

Abraham Van Buren marries Angelica Singleton of South Carolina, who becomes the official hostess of the White House

1839   Border tensions between Americans and Canadians in Maine and New Brunswick

"OK" circulates in Boston newspapers for "oll korrect," soon appropriated by Van Buren reelection campaign

Amistad captured off Long Island

Whig convention at Harrisburg nominates William Henry Harrison and John Tyler

1840   Van Buren issues executive order creating ten-hour workday for federal employees

Pennsylvania Rep. Charles Ogle denounces Van Buren in scathing speech to Congress about White House renovations

Democratic convention meets at Baltimore, renominates Van Buren

Van Buren signs Independent Treasury bill

William Henry Harrison defeats Van Buren

March 1841   William Henry Harrison inaugurated as ninth president

1841   John Quincy Adams wins acquittal of *Amistad* mutineers

Van Buren welcomed in New York City and Kinderhook in tumultuous receptions

1842   Van Buren embarks on extensive tour of southern and western United States; covers 7,000 miles

1844   Van Buren's letter to Mississippi Rep. William Hammet opposes annexation of Texas and immediately jeopardizes his standing in South

Baltimore Democratic convention deadlocks as Southern and Western Democrats reject Van Buren and prevent him from reaching necessary two-thirds support; eventually the dark horse candidate James K. Polk is nominated. Silas Wright rejects the vice presidential nomination, and Northern Democrats are deeply disaffected.

1846–48   Mexican War

1848   Van Buren writes "Barnburner Manifesto" in New York
Democratic convention refuses to seat Barnburner delegation from New York; Barnburners walk out and call for own convention, which nominates Van Buren for presidency on the Free Soil platform; Van Buren receives 291,804 votes (10 percent), enough to swing election to Whig candidate General Zachary Taylor

1853–55   Van Buren travels in Europe

1861   Civil War breaks out and Van Buren supports President Lincoln

July 24, 1862   Martin Van Buren dies at Kinderhook

Selected Bibliography

Adams, John Quincy. *The Memoirs of John Quincy Adams*, ed. Charles Francis Adams (Philadelphia: J. B. Lippincott, 1877).

Alexander, Holmes. *The American Talleyrand: The Career and Contemporaries of Martin Van Buren* (New York: Harper, 1935).

Bancroft, George. *Martin Van Buren to the End of His Public Career* (New York: Harper and Brothers, 1889).

Benton, Thomas Hart. *Thirty Years' View* (New York: D. Appleton and Co., 1854–56).

Binkley, Wilfred E. *American Political Parties: Their Natural History* (New York: Knopf, 1943).

Blue, Frederick J. *The Free Soilers* (Urbana: University of Illinois Press, 1973).

Bruegel, Martin. *Farm, Shop, Landing: The Rise of a Market Society in the Hudson Valley, 1780–1860* (Durham, N.C.: Duke University Press, 2002).

Buckingham, James Silk. *America: Historical, Statistic, and Descriptive* (London: Fisher, Son and Co., 1841).

Burrows, Edwin G., and Mike Wallace. *Gotham: A History of New York City to 1898* (New York: Oxford University Press, 1998).

Butler, William Allen. *Martin Van Buren: Lawyer, Statesman and Man* (New York: D. Appleton, 1862).

———. *A Retrospect of Forty Years* (New York: Charles Scribner's Sons, 1911).

Byrdsall, F. *The History of the Loco-Foco or Equal Rights Party* (New York: Clement and Packard, 1842).

Cole, Donald B. *Martin Van Buren and the American Political System* (Princeton, N.J.: Princeton University Press, 1984).

Crockett, David. *The Life of Martin Van Buren* (Philadelphia: R. Wright, 1835).

Curtis, James C. *The Fox at Bay: Martin Van Buren and the Presidency, 1837–1841* (Lexington: University Press of Kentucky, 1970).

Donovan, Herbert D. A. *The Barnburners: A Study of the Internal Movements in the Political History of New York State and of the Resulting Changes in Political Affiliation, 1830–1852* (New York: New York University Press, 1925).

Emmons, William. *Biography of Martin Van Buren, Vice President of the United States* (Washington, D.C.: J. Gideon, 1835).

Gardiner, O. C. *The Great Issue* (New York: W. C. Bryant & Co., 1848).

Garraty, John Arthur. *Silas Wright* (New York: Columbia University Press, 1949).

Gunderson, Robert Gray. *The Log-Cabin Campaign* (Lexington: University of Kentucky Press, 1957).

Hammond, Jabez D. *The History of Political Parties in the State of New York* (Albany, N.Y.: C. Van Benthuysen, 1842).

Hofstadter, Richard. *The Idea of a Party System* (Berkeley: University of California Press, 1969).

Holland, William M. *The Life and Political Opinions of Martin Van Buren, Vice President of the United States* (Hartford, Conn.: Belknap and Hamersley, 1835).

Hone, Philip. *The Diary of Philip Hone*, ed. Allan Nevins (New York: Dodd, Mead and Company, 1927).

Lynch, Denis Tilden. *An Epoch and a Man* (New York: H. Liveright, 1929).

McCormick, Richard P. *The Second American Party System* (Chapel Hill: University of North Carolina Press, 1966).

McGrane, Reginald C. *The Panic of 1837* (Chicago: University of Chicago Press, 1919).

Merk, Frederick. *Slavery and the Annexation of Texas* (New York: Knopf, 1972).

Mushkat, Jerome, and Rayback, Joseph G. *Martin Van Buren: Law, Politics and the Shaping of Republican Ideology* (De Kalb: Northern Illinois University Press, 1997).

Niven, John. *Martin Van Buren: The Romantic Age of American Politics* (New York: Oxford University Press, 1983).

Remini, Robert. *Martin Van Buren and the Making of the Democratic Party* (New York: Columbia University Press, 1959).

Richards, Leonard L. *The Slave Power: The Free North and Southern Domination, 1780–1860* (Baton Rouge: Louisiana State University Press, 2000).

Schlesinger, Arthur M., Jr. *The Age of Jackson* (Boston: Little, Brown, 1945).

———, ed. *History of U.S. Political Parties* (New York: Chelsea House Publishers, 1973).

Shepard, Edwin M. *Martin Van Buren* (Boston: Houghton Mifflin, 1888).

Sibley, Joel H. *Martin Van Buren and the Emergence of American Popular Politics* (Lanham, Md.: Rowman & Littlefield, 2002).

Strong, George Templeton. *The Diary of George Templeton Strong,* ed. Allan Nevins and Milton Halsey Thomas (New York: Octagon Books, 1952).

Temin, Peter. *The Jacksonian Economy* (New York: Norton, 1969).

Van Buren, Martin. *The Autobiography of Martin Van Buren,* ed. John C. Fitzpatrick (New York: Da Capo Press, 1973 [1920]).

————. *Inquiry into the Origin and Course of Political Parties in the United States* (New York: Hurd and Houghton, 1867).

Weed, Thurlow. *Life of Thurlow Weed Including His Autobiography and a Memoir* (Boston: Houghton Mifflin, 1884).

Wilentz, Sean. *Chants Democratic* (New York: Oxford University Press, 1984).

Wilkes, Charles. *Narrative of the United States Exploring Expedition* (Philadelphia: Lea and Blanchard, 1845).

Wilson, Major L. *The Presidency of Martin Van Buren* (Lawrence: University of Kansas Press, 1984).

Acknowledgments

I would like to thank all the people who provided encouragement of one kind or another during the writing of this book, including Dan Aaron, Bob Allison, Tina Bennett, John Bethell, Alan Brinkley, Doug Brinkley, Alex Chilton, Bill Clinton, Robin Dennis, Henry Louis Gates Jr., Adam Goodheart, Max Kennedy, Thomas LeBien, David Michaelis, Kees de Mooy, Maura Pierce, Mary Rhinelander, Arthur M. Schlesinger Jr., Josh Shenk, Elisabeth Sifton, Jean Sucharewicz, Patricia West, Freddy Widmer, and Sean Wilentz. I am also grateful to the librarians at Harvard University, the Library of Congress, the New York Public Library, and Washington College.

Index

ABOUT THE AUTHOR

Ted Widmer is the director of the C. V. Starr Center for the Study of the American Experience at Washington College. He is the author of *Young America* and the coauthor, with Alan Brinkley, of *Campaigns*. Widmer served as senior adviser to President Clinton and as director of speechwriting at the National Security Council.